Cameos of Christ

Alison Chant

Cameos of Christ
Alison Chant

Copyright Worldwide © 2009 by Alison Chant

ISBN: 978-1-61529-193-9

All rights reserved worldwide

No part of this book may be reproduced in any manner without the written permission of the author except in brief quotes embodied in critical articles or reviews.

Vision Publishing
P.O. Box 1680
Ramona, CA 92065
1 (760) 789-4700
www.booksbyvision.org

All scripture quotes from the New International Version unless otherwise stated.

Other books in print

Unsung Heroines - A Manual for Pastors' Wives

Divine Healing – The Wonder and the Mystery

Walking in the Spirit

Dedication

This book is dedicated to
Dale, Sharon, Eric and Baden

Table of Contents

Foreword 7

Preface 9

    Many wonderful things are noted about Jesus.

Chapter One: The Reality of Jesus 11

    Jesus of Nazareth, the Messiah, is mentioned in the history books. The Messiah's lineage is discussed. The witnesses to Jesus pre-existence are listed and the theophanies, including the role of the Angel of his Presence, is explored.

Chapter Two: Jesus Is The Only Way 27

    Jesus is the only way. The proof of genuine prophecy is in its fulfilment and God's remarkably accurate foreknowledge proves his sovereignty. Prophetic paradoxes from Jesus life were solved easily.

Chapter Three: Prophetic Details 41

    Prophecies are listed concerning Jesus birth, life, character, dual nature, death and resurrection. One of Daniel's prophecies gives the exact timing of both Jesus ministry and his death. Jesus' ministry is predicted and confirmed.

Chapter Four: The Fascination of Typology 61

    Typology is defined here and care has been taken to teach that types are meant to amplify doctrine not to originate it. Some of the more obvious types are explored.

Chapter Five: Cameos Of Christ 79

    God's wonderful plan is outlined. Types from the Tabernacle are examined and the connections to John's gospel are noted. The incense used on the altar of incense is explored.

Chapter Six: Pictures Of Christ 93

Pictures of Christ examined through various Old Testament saints increasing our understanding of Christ.

Chapter Seven: Types of Christ.. 105

More Old Testament types reveal more of Christ

Chapter Eight: Saviour, Shepherd and Sovereign..................... 115

A trilogy of Messianic Psalms revealing three aspects of Christ.

Chapter Nine: Christ in Isaiah 123

Showing the stunning breadth of Isaiah's vision of the Messiah.

Chapter Ten: Bible Portraits.. 133

A list of Old Testament books that portray Christ in various aspects of his life and ministry.

Chapter Eleven: More Bible Portraits 145

The remaining books of the Old Testament reveal more wonders of Christ.

Chapter Twelve: The Claims of Jesus 155

He laid aside his godhead. He challenged the Jews. He showed his great authority. He established his uniqueness. He proved his claim to be the Son of God by his healing and deliverance ministry. He chose his disciples well and they gave eye witness testimony to his bodily resurrection.

Chapter Thirteen: Jesus The One and Only Son 165

Five word pictures of Jesus on which to reflect. The Creator, the Holy One, the Compassionate Healer, the Mighty Redeemer, and the Resurrection and the Life.

Addendum One: Christ In All The Scriptures 173
Addendum Two 181
    Some helpful books that support the supremacy of the original four gospels Matthew, Mark, Luke and John.
Bibliography 183

Foreword

Old Testament prophecies and types are fascinating for anyone eager to follow the unveiling of the life of Jesus found there and this book is the result of many years of research and teaching on this subject.

I thank God for the many reputable scholars who have wrought with the Word of God over the last 2,000 years of church history. This has resulted in a rich tapestry of Christian thought that can be drawn on by modern teachers who can then add their own insights and understanding to the foundation built by those who have gone before.

My determination to put down the things I have learned has kept me writing through almost three years. I have prayed for insight and understanding and the Lord has revealed some treasures that seem new and wonderful to me. We are told that there is nothing new under the sun, but there are new ways of telling the story of Jesus and this is what I have attempted to do.

You may ask why the name Cameos of Christ? A cameo is a picture of a raised profile of a head and shoulders carved from an agate or perhaps a carnelian stone. It is usually worn as a brooch or a pendant and can be the profile of a man or a woman. The ideas established in this book convey a portrait of Christ, raised up in profile, like a cameo, from the pages of the Old Testament through accurate prophecy and fascinating type.

I am aware there are many books of this type already in print but in these days of increasing secularism I wanted my own family to have answers for the mockers; a firm foundation for their own faith in God.

I pray that all those who study this book will open up their hearts and lives to Jesus more fully, worshipping him in all his splendour as the One and Only Son of the Living God.

Alison Chant

Preface

In the life of Jesus we can identify many remarkable discoveries. What a fascinating person he was in his incarnation, when he walked here on earth among his people. One particular verse in the gospel of Mark reveals the incredible excitement he aroused in the crowds of people who followed him –

> *As soon as all the people saw Jesus, they were overwhelmed with wonder and ran to greet him* (Mark 9:15).

What was the background of this incident? Jesus had just come down from Mount Tabor where he had been transfigured (Mark 9:1-7). There is no other explanation for the wonder of the people. Jesus must have been trailing clouds of heaven's glory! Something of his experience still clung to him. He still emanated the power and the presence of God to such an extent that the people wondered at it.

There were many times the disciples viewed him with awe. They were amazed at Jesus power in rebuking the storm on the Sea of Galilee and they cried out –

> *'What kind of man is this? Even the winds and the sea obey him!'* (Matthew 8:27)

Those who have studied the Bible know who he is. He is the Word of God become flesh, the One and Only Son who came from the Father, full of grace and truth (John1:14)

He is the Lamb of God who takes away our sin and brings us into eternal life. If we receive him we know we have the right to become children of God (John 1:12-13).

He is the great teacher who taught with the authority received from his Father. He knew how to reach ordinary people, how to explain God to them. They were fascinated by his wisdom (Matthew 22:15-21).

He describes himself as the Shepherd of his people, and as the Gate through which they must enter into eternal life (John 10:7-11); as the Light of the world (John 8:12) and the Bread which came down from heaven (John 6:35-40). He is all these things and more.

He was born holy, without sin, and he remained holy throughout his life and ministry so that he could become the perfect sacrifice for our sin.

He was always obedient and submissive to his Father –

> *'The one who sent me is with me; he has not left me alone, for I always do what pleases him'* (John 8:29).

He was anointed to heal the sick and to set free those who were bound (Isaiah 61:1) and he went about doing good and healing all who were oppressed in any way by Satan, for God was with him (Acts 10:38).

He was full of compassion and pity for the multitude (Matthew 9:35-36) yet stern with those who led the people astray with their onerous laws (23:1-36). He was courageous in the face of a terrible death knowing his Father would not leave him or forsake him but raise him up again in victory (Psalm 16:9-10).

Right through the Old Testament this same Jesus appears. Time and time again, in prophecy and type his portrait stands out in bold and dazzling relief, creating a beautiful cameo, convincing us that truly he is the Son of the Living God.

Before we begin exploring the proofs of the identity of Jesus may I humbly suggest to those who are still seeking the truth: 'Take heed to the wise words of Jeremiah the prophet' –

> *This is what the Lord says, 'Let not the wise man boast of his wisdom or the strong man boast of his strength or the rich man boast of his riches, but let him who boasts boast about this: that he understands and knows me, that I am the Lord who exercises kindness justice and righteousness on earth, for in these I delight,' declares the Lord* (Jeremiah 9:23-24).

Chapter One:

The Reality of Jesus

Jesus in History

Jesus is well documented in history books. Beside the authors of the New Testament he is mentioned by two contemporary historians, Josephus (a Jew) and Tacitus (a Roman). Both these men wrote histories for their respective countries. The remarks by Josephus are sympathetic but the remarks by Tacitus show his heathen beliefs. He had little understanding of Christianity.

Josephus published *Antiquities of the Jews* in AD 93. The following quote comes from Book 18, Chapter 3, Item 3, which in the translation by William Whiston reads –

> At this time there appeared Jesus, a wise man, if it be lawful to call him a man; for he was a doer of wonderful works, a teacher of such men as receive the truth with pleasure. He drew over to him both many of the Jews and many of the Gentiles. He was (the) Christ. And when Pilate, at the suggestion of the principal men amongst us, had condemned him to the cross, those that loved him at the first did not forsake him; for he appeared to them alive again the third day; as the divine prophets had foretold these and ten thousand other wonderful things concerning him. And the tribe of Christians, so named from him, are not extinct to this day.[1]

Some scholars believe that Christians added to Josephus' passage, but the fact remains that Jesus was mentioned by him.

---

[1] This quote, from Josephus, known as the *Testimonium Flavianum*, has been the subject of debate since the 17th century.

The next historical quote, this time from Tacitus, concerns the fire of Rome possibly started by the Emperor Nero who wanted to build a new city. He blamed the Christians for the fire and persecuted them to hide his guilt. Remember Tacitus was not a Christian and he did not understand anything about Jesus, so he too blames the Christians for the fire. He refers to Jesus as Christus, the Latin form of the word 'Christ' –

> But, despite kindly influence, despite the leader's generous handouts, despite appeasing the gods, the scandal did not subside, rather the blaze came to be believed to be an official act. So, in order to quash the rumour, Nero blamed it on, and applied the cruellest punishments to, those sinners, whom ordinary people call Christians, hating them for their shameful behaviour. The originator of this name, Christus, was sent to execution by Procurator Pontius Pilate, during the reign of Tiberius.[2]

These two quotes which originate from outside the New Testament are sufficient to establish the fact that Jesus was a real person, a historical figure and not a myth as some would have us believe.

The New Testament, with its four gospels, powerfully describes the birth of Jesus, his life and ministry, and his death, resurrection and ascension back into heaven.

Recent Scholarship

Within the last few years there have been many scholars who have weakened the faith of some Christians with their contention that the four gospels in the New Testament are not the only books we should look to for facts about Jesus. They have cited gospels, such as the *Gospel of Thomas*, which were not accepted by the early church fathers as genuine. These other gospels were written over one hundred or more years after the crucifixion and resurrection of

---

[2] Tacitus; Roman historian; *Annals;* Concerning the Great Fires of Rome (c. AD116).

Jesus and they show a strong Gnostic influence. They are not eye witness accounts as are the four gospels, *Matthew, Mark, Luke* and *John.* Slowly but surely the men who have made false claims about Jesus from these spurious gospels have been shown up as shallow and lacking in true scholarship by other more reputable scholars such as Craig A. Evans (Ph.D.) Evans was a professor for twenty years at Trinity Western University where he directed the graduate programmes in biblical studies and founded the Dead Sea Scrolls Institute. He is interviewed by Lee Strobel in his book *The Case for the Real Jesus,* and during their conversation Evans is well able to eliminate these later gospels. I have cited this book and the books of other scholars who have written to support the supremacy of the four original gospels in 'Addendum Two'.

Jesus in Scripture

Why did Jesus come into this world? There were two main reasons. One was to show us what God was truly like. Those who point to God's apparent cruelty in the Old Testament stories do not understand that the early prophets only saw glimpses of God and did not understand him in his fullness. Jesus came to rectify this misunderstanding; to show us that God is love and has compassion for his creation (John 14:9). As Dr. William Barclay points out in his commentary on John 1:1 –

> If the Word was with God before time began, if God's Word is part of the eternal scheme of things, it means that God was always like Jesus. Sometimes we tend to think of God as just and holy and stern and avenging; and we tend to think that something that Jesus did changed God's anger into love, and altered God's attitude to men. The New Testament knows nothing of that idea. The whole New Testament tells us, and this passage in John, specially tells us, that God has always

been like Jesus. What Jesus did was open a window in time that we might see the eternal and unchanging love of God.[3]

The other and primary reason Jesus came was to be the sacrifice for all mankind. All those who accept him as Saviour become part of God's family (John 1:12; 3:16).

Slowly, as he grew and matured, Jesus became aware of his destiny. At the age of twelve he said to his parents, *'Don't you know I must be about my Father's business?* Well before his thirtieth year he knew who he was; he knew why he was born and what his ministry and final sacrifice would accomplish. He had studied the Old Testament scriptures and knew the prophecies concerning himself were being fulfilled exactly as had been foretold; he saw himself in David's cry –

> *Then I said, 'Here I am, I have come – it is written about me in the scroll. I desire to do your will, O my God; your law is within my heart'* (Psalm 40:7-8).

Jesus said (referring to the Old Testament)

> *'These are the scriptures that testify about me'* (John 5:39b).

Here are some of these scriptures –

He was to be the seed of the woman (Genesis 3:15). When Adam and Eve fell into disobedience and were expelled from the Garden of Eden, God promised them that one day a Redeemer would come. He was to be the seed of the woman, and this unusual phrase indicates he would be born without an earthly father. He was to crush the head of the serpent, thus overcoming the power of Satan forever. In turn the serpent was to bruise his heel. From our perspective, thousands of years later, a glimpse can be caught of the manner of the Redeemer's death as he allowed himself to be sacrificed on a cross for our salvation.

---

[3] Barclay, William; *The Daily Study Bible*; 'The Gospel of John', Volume One; St. Andrew Press Edinburgh; 1962. Pg. 15.

He was to be descended from Abraham (Genesis 22:18). Abraham was the friend of God because of his steadfast faith. He believed that God would grant him a son through his wife Sarah even though it was impossible in the natural because of their great age. Because of his faith he was accounted righteous before God (Romans 4:18-22). Due to his obedience later on in being willing to offer that same son, Isaac, to God (Genesis 22:1-12) Abraham was promised that through his offspring all the earth would be blessed. So Jesus, the redeemer to come, was to be descended from Abraham.

He was to come through the tribe of Judah (Genesis 49:8-10). When Judah was given Israel's final blessing he was given a prophecy that the sceptre would not depart from Judah, nor the ruling staff from between his feet. In Revelation Jesus is given the name, *The Lion of the tribe of Judah* (Revelation 5:5). God has exalted him now to the highest office and one day every knee will bow and every tongue confess that he is King of kings and Lord of lords (Isaiah 45:22-24a; Revelation 19:11-16)

He was to be of the family of David (Psalm 89:3-4). David was a man after God's own heart, a prophet who saw into the future; the sweet psalmist who ruled as king over Israel. David came from the tribe of Judah and Jesus was to be from the family of David. In *Revelation* he is called the *Root of David* (Revelation 5:5). The prophet Jeremiah also foretold that Jesus would come from the family of David -

> *'The days are coming,' declares the Lord, 'when I will raise up to David a righteous branch, a King who will reign wisely and do what is just and right in the land. In his days Judah will be saved, and Israel will live in safety. This is the name by which he will be called: The Lord Our Righteousness'* (Jeremiah 23:5-6; see also 33:15-16).

He was to be born of a virgin (Isaiah 7:14). The maiden too was to be of the family of David. Mary was the one chosen and approved. She was bravely willing to face the gossip and danger of this choice to be God's handmaiden (Luke 1:26-38).

He was to be called Wonderful, Counsellor, Mighty God, Prince of Peace (Isaiah 9:2-7). Some of the prophecies of the Old Testament are hard to understand and this is one of them, for how could the Chosen One be the Mighty God as well as the Prince of Peace? How could he be the Everlasting Father as well as the Son? Now of course we can understand these seeming paradoxes as Jesus in his incarnation had two natures. He was without limitation or diminution God and yet also wholly man.

His ministry was to be one of healing, restoration and deliverance (Isaiah 61:1-3; Malachi 4:2). The Messiah to come was to be anointed for a very special task. He was to heal, to restore, to deliver, to set the captives free, to open the eyes of the blind and to comfort those who mourn. These abilities were in part his credentials proving he was the Son of God, the Messiah, who had been promised (Acts 10:38).

He was to die on a cross (Psalm 22; Isaiah 53). He was to be sacrificed for the salvation of mankind, freely giving himself for our salvation. Truly he deserves our full faithful obedience.

He was to rise again from the dead (Psalm 16:10). No one had ever spontaneously risen from the dead before Jesus. No one believed it was possible. Even though Jesus told the disciples over and over again that he was destined to die on a cross and then rise on the third day (Matthew16:21; 17:23; 20:19), they could not believe, nor remotely understand, how this could be. But this is what did happen and here in the Psalms the event is recorded as a prophecy a thousand years before its fulfilment. God knows the end from the beginning: he decreed that Jesus was to rise again from the dead and nothing could stop this from happening.

The Lineage of Jesus

Jesus was born into this world through Abraham's family and indeed Jesus' ancestry, listed for us in Matthew, is a fascinating one. We see there are women mentioned who are Gentiles (Rahab the Caananite and Ruth the Moabite), and two others who committed adultery (Tamar and Bathsheba), indicating that the gentiles and repentant sinners are to be included in Jesus' kingdom family. There are some gaps in Matthew's list but it was common practice for the Jews to leave out any ancestors they considered not worth mentioning.

This list in Matthew and the list given by Luke are different. Matthew may have traced the lineage of Joseph who would be identified as the lawful, earthly father of Jesus, and Luke the lineage of Mary who was the mother of Jesus. The reverse could also be true, as Matthew's list includes Mary but Luke does not mention her. Both came from the family of David and proof of this would have been available from the temple records. A good Bible dictionary will give a full explanation of the genealogies of Jesus: Here is one quote from Nelson's –

> For Matthew, the unfolding of Israelite history revealed Christ the Messiah, whose coming issued in the age of grace, Luke's list reflects a wider concern by portraying Christ as the Saviour of all peoples; not just the Jews. By reversing the normal order of listing Luke may have intended to demonstrate the real nature of Jesus as the divine Son.[4]

Albert Barnes maintains that –

> No difficulty was ever found, or alleged, in regard to (the genealogies) by any of the early enemies of Christianity. There is no evidence that they ever adduced them as containing a contradiction. Many of those enemies were acute, learned, and able; and they show by their writings that

---

[4] Youngblood, Ronald F. General Editor; Bruce, F.F. and Harrison, R.K. Consulting Editors; *Nelson's New Illustrated Bible Dictionary;* Reference: 'The Genealogies of Jesus'; Thomas Nelson Publishers; 1995.

they were not indisposed to detect all the errors that could possibly be found in the sacred narrative.[5]

Joseph and Mary came from a poor part of the family of David. Joseph was a carpenter, working with his hands to earn their daily bread. This confirms the prophecy that the Messiah would come like a stump out of dry ground, from the lowest and poorest part of the family of David, yet still the blood of the king ran in their veins (Isaiah 11:1; 53:2).

The Pharisees and Teachers Are Mistaken

Even though his lineage could not be disputed (because Jesus' birth was registered in the temple) the Jewish leaders were confused as to his identity. They were unable to refute the fact that he was born in Bethlehem from the family of David, yet they refused to accept him as their Messiah. They were blind as to the purpose of God as the prophecies concerning the Messiah were of both his first coming as a suffering Saviour, and his second coming as a conquering King.

The Jews were expecting their Messiah to be a powerful ruler who would rid them of the Roman legions and return them to the glory the nation had enjoyed under David and Solomon. They did not understand that Jesus had to first suffer on the cross and later return as King of kings.

The prophets who spoke of the Messiah were shown his first coming and his second coming as two future mountain ranges and were unaware that there would be a long valley of time between the two events.

Jewish leaders were eager to believe Zechariah's prophecy of the Messiah's kingship but they were blinded to Isaiah's prophecy of his suffering and death. In comparing the following two scriptures you will be able to see and understand their blindness. They had a

---

[5] Barnes, Albert; *Notes on the New Testament*; Kregel Publications; Grand Rapids; Michigan; 1966. Pg. 2.

similar problem in their day, as we do now, as we try to understand the prophecies concerning the second coming of Christ –

> *On that day his feet will stand on the Mount of Olives, east of Jerusalem* (Zechariah 14:4). *The Lord will be king over the whole earth. On that day there will be one Lord, and his name the only name* (14:9).
>
> *But he was pierced for our transgressions. He was crushed for our iniquities; the punishment that brought us peace was upon him, and by his wounds we are healed* (Isaiah 53:5).

On the Road to Emmaus

Luke tells the intriguing story of two of Jesus' disciples meeting the risen Christ on the road to Emmaus (Luke 24:13-35). One of these two was Cleopas (or Alpheus), the father of the apostles James and Jude (also named James and Thaddeus in Matthew 10:2-3). Some ancient manu-scripts name Cleopas as brother to Joseph the husband of Mary (the mother of Jesus) making James and Thaddeus cousins of Jesus. The other disciple is not named. Neither were from the twelve disciples, but were probably two of the seventy who had previously been sent out by Jesus to preach about the kingdom and heal the sick (Luke 10:1-17). It appears certain that some New Testament Bible char-acters have more than one name in English so there is some confusion also in deciphering the names of a few of the other disciples but the research has been done for us by scholars such as John Gill, Albert Barnes, and F. F. Bruce. [6]

Emmaus was seven miles from Jerusalem, so after joining Cleopas and his companion Jesus had two or three hours while they walked and talked together to make the scriptures clear to them. Beginning

---

[6] Gill, John. *Exposition of the Entire Bible*. E Sword; Reference: Luke 24:18: 'And one of them, whose name was Cleophas,... Or Alphaeus, for it is the same name; he was one of the seventy disciples, and father of the Apostles James and Jude, and brother to Joseph, the husband of Mary, the mother of Christ, as before observed.'

with Moses he pointed out that all the scriptures concerning himself had been fulfilled. He showed them that his life was clearly foretold in the Law of Moses, in the Prophets and in the Psalms, as we too shall see in further chapters of this book (Luke 24:25-27; 44-45).

During his earthly ministry Jesus referred to various Old Testament characters and quoted from many different books in the Hebrew scriptures (John 8:56; Matthew 12:39-42; 22:41-46). He knew the Old Testament thoroughly and its testimony concerning his virgin birth, his compassionate life, his painful death and his victorious resurrection.

Jesus' Pre-Existence

In English we have only singular and plural terms; Hebrew has forms for singular, dual, and plural. In Genesis 1:1, the first verse of the Bible, the Hebrew word for God, *Elohim,* is cast in the plural. This word for God is used around 2,500 times throughout the Old Testament scriptures (see Genesis 1:26; cp. Colossians 1:16-17).[7]

This fact is one of the Bible proofs of the Trinity, the fact that Father, Son, and Holy Spirit encompass the God-head. There are other indications of the Trinity in scripture: one is found in Isaiah's call to be God's messenger which reads in part, '*Whom shall I send and who will go for us?*'(Isaiah 6:8)

There are many more witnesses to the fact of Christ's pre-existence:

The witness of the Lord in the beginning: *Then God said, 'Let us make man in our own image, in our likeness'* (Genesis 1:26a).

---

[7] Christians are quick to note this and wonder why the Jewish people do not see it. Some commentators presume that the Jews consider that these verses are using the royal plural rather than indicating the Trinity; Father, Son and Holy Spirit in which Christians believe.

The witness of the Lord at the Tower of Babel: *'Come, let us go down and confuse their language so they will not understand each other'* (Genesis 11:7).

The witness of John the Baptist: *'A man who comes after me has surpassed me because he was before me'* (John 1:30b).

The witness of Christ's own words: *'Before Abraham was born I am!'* (John 8:58b).

The witness of John the beloved disciple: *In the beginning was the Word and the Word was with God, and the Word was God. He was with God in the beginning... (John1:1-2). That which was from the beginning, which we have heard, which we have seen with our eyes, which we have looked at and our hands have touched – this we proclaim concerning the Word of life.* (1 John 1:1).

The witness on the Mount of Transfiguration. Jesus revealed to his disciples Peter, James and John the glory that was his, and Moses and Elijah appeared and spoke with him concerning his coming death and resurrection. Moses represented the Law and Elijah the Prophets. *There he was transfigured before them. His face shone like the sun, and his clothes became white as the light. Just then there appeared before them Moses and Elijah, talking with Jesus* (Matthew 17:2-3).

The witness of Peter. Along with James and John Peter saw Jesus' glory on Mt. Tabor: *He (Jesus) was chosen before the creation of the world, but was revealed in these last times for your sake* (1 Peter 1:20). *We did not follow cleverly invented stories when we told you about the power and coming of our Lord Jesus Christ, but we were eyewitnesses of his majesty. For he received honour and glory from God the Father when the voice came to him from the Majestic Glory, saying 'This is my Son, whom I love, with him I am well pleased'* (2 Peter 1:16-17).

The witness of Paul the apostle: *He is the image of the invisible God, the firstborn over all creation. For by him were all things created (*Colossians 1:15-16a). *Who being in very nature God, did* *not consider equality with God something to be grasped* (Philippians 2:6).

The witness of the writer to the Hebrews: *But in these last days he has spoken to us by his Son, whom he appointed heir of all things, and through whom he made the universe. The Son is the radiance of God's glory, and the exact representation of his being, sustaining all things by his powerful word* (Hebrews 1:2-3a).

The Theophanies

A theophany is a visible appearance of God in Old Testament times. Jesus is referred to as the visible expression of God (Hebrews 1:3) and as the Word of God (John 1:1) and this infers that it was Jesus from whom Adam and Eve hid when they heard the sound (or the voice) of the Lord God walking in the garden of Eden (Genesis 3:8).

Enoch (Genesis 5:21-24) and Noah (Genesis 6:8-9) also walked with God. Abraham had an experience of the physical presence of God by the oak tree at Mamre where he pleaded for the citizens of Sodom and Gomorrah (Genesis 18). Joshua also definitely saw a physical appearance (Joshua 5:13-15). This must have been a theophany because he was told to take off his sandals as the place on which he was standing was holy ground.

Others heard God's voice but saw no physical manifestation.

The Angel of His Presence

Isaiah talks of the 'angel of his presence' being a Saviour and a Redeemer. *In all their distress he too was distressed, and the <u>angel of his presence</u> saved them. In his love and mercy he redeemed them; he lifted them up and carried them all the days of old* (Isaiah 63: 9).

Hagar, Sara's handmaid and the mother of Ishmael, named the angel of the Lord, *'the God who sees me,'* (Genesis 16: 13-14). Beer Lahai Roi, the well where the angel of the Lord found Hagar, is translated *'The well of the Living One who sees me.'*

When Abraham was about to sacrifice Isaac upon the altar it was the angel of the Lord who spoke to him indicating by the text that the angel of the Lord and Christ in his pre-existence are one and the same.

> *But the angel of the Lord called out to him from heaven. 'Abraham! Abraham!' 'Here I am', he replied. 'Do not lay a hand on the boy', he said, 'Do not do anything to him. Now I know that you fear God, <u>because you have not withheld from me your son, your only son</u>'* (Genesis 22:11-12).

He appeared to Jacob and wrestled with him s*o Jacob called the place Peniel, saying, 'It is because I saw God face to face, and yet my life was spared'* (Genesis 32:30).

The angel of the Lord accompanied Eliezer on his journey to find a wife for Isaac (Genesis 24:7).

It was the angel of the Lord who was in the burning bush and revealed himself to Moses as, *'The God of your father, the God of Abraham, the God of Isaac and the God of Jacob'* (Exodus 3:6a) and as, *'I AM WHO I AM'* (Exodus 3:14a).

He guided the children of Israel to their promised land and talked to Moses giving him the Ten Commandments on Mt Sinai (Exodus 13:21-22; 14:19; Chapters 19 and 20).

He blocked the road before Balaam on his covetous mission to curse the people of Israel for gain (Numbers 22:22).

In Exodus God promises an angel to go before Moses and the people of Israel. He says, *'Pay attention to him and listen to what he says. Do not rebel against him; he will not forgive your rebellion, since my Name is in him'* (Exodus 23:21).

The angel of the Lord appeared also to Gideon and instructed him in what to do to overcome the Midianites. Note that he accepted Gideon's offering, a sacrifice belonging only to God (Judges 6:11-24).

Manoah and his wife spoke with the angel of the Lord when they were told of the coming birth of Samson. When they offered a sacrifice and the angel of the Lord ascended in the flames Manoah cried out *'We are doomed to die! We have seen God!'* (Judges 13:22).

When Elijah fled to Beer Sheba and journeyed further into the desert by himself he was in despair, wanting to die after the effort and the triumph of Mt Carmel and the killing of the prophets of Baal. The angel of the Lord was very understanding. He gave him bread to eat and water to drink then allowed him to rest before he spoke to him. He then chose Elisha as a companion and helper for Elijah and challenged him to go on to a new commission (1Kings 19:1-21).

In many of these instances the angel of the Lord and the Voice of the Lord and the Word of the Lord are used interchangeably which indicates that the angel of the Lord mentioned in the Old Testament was indeed the Christ in his pre-existence.

In two of these instances (Manoah and Gideon) the angel of the Lord accepts sacrificial offerings which belong only to God himself.

Conclusion

The view of most Bible teachers is that the angel of the Lord is a distinct personal manifestation of God, the incarnate Logos (John 1:1). In other words the angel of the Lord was Jesus himself, in the glory that was his before he allowed himself to be born as a tiny babe in Bethlehem. To permit this he emptied himself, putting aside his glory and his power, a process in theology called the *'kenosis'* of Christ (Philippians 2:5-11).

The angel of the Lord is unique and distinct from other angels. He appears as God and yet distinct from God. He spoke to the Old Testament characters, person to person, indicating what God wanted them to do.

In contrast to these appearances the angel of Revelation 19:9-10 refused worship and proclaimed himself to be a fellow servant with John.

Chapter Two:

Jesus Is The Only Way

Many modern thinkers, with their miscellany of beliefs and their refusal to accept the absolute truth of the gospel are questioning that Jesus is the only way to God. They see other religions all around them, other ways of thinking and believing, and they say to themselves, 'Why do Christians insist that Jesus Christ is the only way to heaven?'

But the New Testament states without equivocation that Jesus is indeed the only way!

> *Salvation is found in no one else, for there is no other name under heaven given to men by which we must be saved* (Acts 4:12). *For there is one God and one mediator between God and men, the man Christ Jesus, who gave himself as a ransom for all men* (1 Timothy 2:5-6a).

Jesus is the unique sacrifice who brings forgiveness for sin and makes humanity fit for heaven. He came to reveal the love and mercy of God. Having completed the task of salvation he is now seated on the right hand of God, as the writer to the Hebrews makes clear–

> *In the past God spoke to our forefathers through the prophets at many times and in various ways, but in these last days he has spoken to us by his Son, whom he appointed heir of all things, and through whom he made the universe. The Son is the radiance of God's glory and the exact representation of his being, sustaining all things by his powerful word. After he had provided purification for sins, he sat down at the right hand of the majesty in heaven* (Hebrews 1:1-3).

No other religion offers forgiveness for all our sin and eternal life that cannot be bought with money. The Lord, through Isaiah, urges us to grasp hold of that free salvation –

> *Come, all you who are thirsty, come to the waters; and you who have no money, come, buy and eat! Come buy wine and milk without money and without cost. Give ear and come to me; hear me that your soul may live. I will make an everlasting covenant with you* (Isaiah 55: 1-3).

Prophecy and Pattern

The Old Testament contains through prophecy and type a striking mosaic of patterns that point to Christ. Out of these prophecies and types a beautiful picture of Christ arises which proves his claim to be the Son of God. The oracles portray his birth, his life, his character, his ministry gifts and the milestones of his earthly ministry. If the New Testament had not been written we would have great difficulty understanding the Old Testament. The New Testament shows us the life of Jesus and thus the fulfilment of all the prophecies concerning the Saviour that are clearly outlined in the Old Testament.

The Eastern Mind-Set

To better understand the Bible it is helpful to study the mind-set of eastern peoples, who are similar to the Jews of Bible days. In eastern thinking there is a separation between the things of the spirit and the things of science and reason. Eastern people are able to hold scientific beliefs that require logical thinking, and at the same time to hold contrary religious beliefs. They see nothing strange in this. The western mind on the other hand wants to understand and work out all aspects of belief and as a result their scholars tend to write systematic theologies in which they endeavour to make the doctrines of the Bible fully consistent and coherent.

However, God has ordained that reason and philosophy cannot and will not reveal Jesus (1Corinthians 1:18-25). He must first be accepted by faith. Only then will God pour out his grace and mercy on us so that we gain the revelation and understanding we need through his Word (1 Corinthians 2:6-16).

In the beginning God had a plan. Before the foundation of the world he knew that people would fall into disobedience and he made provision for this (Ephesians 1:3-14). From the moment Adam and Eve left the Garden of Eden he determined that there would be an accurate prophetic record to portray the future life of Jesus.

In time he chose a man, Abraham, and from this man, through generations of people came the nation Israel. That nation had to be refined and prepared for the moment when the Christ, the Lamb of God, would appear. Slowly but surely God's plan unfolded and each step was written down and preserved, sometimes as prophecy but also in types, so that no one would be able to say God did not know and plan every aspect of the life of his Son.

Because of their eastern mind-set the Rabbis (Jewish teachers) of old were able to take giant steps from one idea to another, even though it might appear at first that there was no connection. We can see this illustrated in some of the prophecies that Matthew refers to as proofs that Jesus is the Son of God.

In Exodus 4:22 The Lord calls Israel his first born son and then in Hosea 11:1 the prophet writes: *When Israel was a child, I loved him, and out of Egypt I called my son.*

Matthew draws our attention to Hosea to explain that God knew beforehand Jesus' parents would have to flee with him to Egypt. God brought his people Israel out of Egypt and into the land he had promised; he also kept Jesus safe with his parents in Egypt, bringing him out when the danger had past.

Then there is the prophecy concerning the murder of the children. The women of Jeremiah's time suffered the death of their little ones, just as the mothers of Bethlehem would suffer the same agony in the future –

> *A voice is heard in Ramah, weeping and great mourning, Rachel weeping for her children and refusing to be comforted, because they are no more* (Matthew 2:18)

Matthew claims that this prophecy, originally from Jeremiah 31:15, was not only for that day but also for the time when Herod, in his anxiety to get rid of the threat to his throne, ordered the murder of the infant boys in and around Bethlehem.

From those two instances we can conclude that some prophecies may have a first and a second fulfilment, and sometimes even more.

The Prophets

As we study the prophecies we become aware that there are glimpses, images, and oracles throughout the Old Testament that give us an overall picture of the wonder of Christ and his life, ministry, death, resurrection and ascension into heaven's glory. The foreknowledge of God is awe inspiring and anyone who can grasp the accuracy and detail of the prophecies concerning Jesus will be convinced that God planned it all. Indeed the proofs are so accurate that only those who are determined not to believe can refuse the solid evidence. Here is what God has to say through his prophet Isaiah concerning the future –

> *I am God and there is no other; I am God, and there is none like me; I make known the end from the beginning, from ancient times, what is still to come. I say my purpose will stand and I will do all that I please* (Isaiah 46:9b-10).

Moses outlined the test of a true prophet in Deuteronomy 18:21-22.

> *You may say to yourselves, 'How can we know when a message has not been spoken by the Lord?' If what a prophet proclaims in the name of the lord does not take place or come true, that is a message the Lord has not spoken. That prophet spoke presumptuously. Do not be afraid of him.*

Here is what Dr. A. T. Pierson has to say about genuine prophets and their oracles about the future found in the Bible:

> Predictive prophecy is the foremost proof to which the Word of God appeals on its own behalf. It was the standing miracle by which God challenged faith in his inspired Word, defying all the worshipers of other gods and their sages and peers to produce any such proofs that their gods were worthy of worship or their prophets true representatives of a Divine religion. [8]

The Old Testament prophets came from many different walks of life and they were very different from one another in temperament, but even so they were all used by God. Elijah the Tishbite came from the wilderness across the Jordan, wore rough clothing with a leather belt (2 Kings 1:8), and had no fixed abode. Through his many prayers he shook the nation of Israel and destroyed the priests of Baal. In contrast Isaiah was of the ruling class and had access to the king whenever he needed to speak to him. He was a poet as well as a prophet, and of all the prophets he had most to say about the Messiah who was to come.

Some were rich men, some poor farmers, some were women, but all of them had a deep personal faith and when they received a word from God, they spoke with great power and anointing.

In the Old Testament, in contrast to the priest who spoke to God for the people, the prophet was a preacher, a spokesman for God, one who declared by divine inspiration something that would take place, sometimes immediately, but sometimes far into the future. This kind of prophetic office was different from anything we might experience today. The Old Testament prophets knew without any doubt they were speaking as God's messenger and they held fiercely to the words they were given, even to the point of death. and many of them did die at the hands of wicked men (2 Kings 9:7;

---

[8] Pierson, A. T. *The Scriptures:* 'God's Living Oracles'; Pickering and Inglis; London; 1904.

Jeremiah 26:20-23). However, they were not perfect, and sometimes they failed, as Elijah did after his great victory on Mt Carmel against the priests of Baal (1 Kings 19:3-4). Had Elijah continued to defy King Ahab and his wife Jezebel perhaps he may have turned the whole country back to God. As it was he was overcome by Jezebel's furious threats and collapsed into despair.

In the New Testament the office of prophet is different and the New Testament word for prophet means to 'speak forth' or 'forth teller'. New Testament prophecy has in it more of the idea of strengthening, comforting, and encouragement rather than the foretelling of future events (1 Corinthians 14:3).

Nowadays the foretelling of future events in a person's life can sometimes happen through what is called 'personal prophecy', but this type of prophecy needs to be treated with great caution. A Christian will usually find that the word given is a confirmation of something God has already revealed to him from another source. If not then it is better to wait for further confirmation before acting on a 'personal prophecy'. This will ensure that no life-destroying mistakes are made as we are advised in scripture –.

> *A matter must be established by the testimony of two or three witnesses* (Deuteronomy 19:15b). *Many advisers make victory sure* (Proverbs 11:14b).

Isaiah explains that unless the person prophesying is a genuine prophet, speaking according to the Word of God, then you cannot trust what they say. A prophecy must never disagree with God's word already revealed in scripture, for in God there is no shadow of turning, he does not change from day to day (James 1:17). The life and character of the prophet must also measure up to God's standard of holiness and purity, Jesus himself tells us to watch out for false prophets, and that we will know them by the life they live and by the fruit they bear (Matthew 7:15-20).

As we study the Old Testament for the treasures we can unearth we must ask the Holy Spirit to give us revelation (John 14:16-17; 15:26; 16:13-15). Be sure that our meditation will be pleasing to

God who wants all his children to know the truth. As we hold to the teachings of Jesus it is the truth of scripture that sets us free (John 8:31-32). The Lord knows those who love and respect him and honour his name, those who search after the truth, as we are told in Malachi –

> *'Then those who feared the Lord talked with each other, and the Lord listened and heard. A scroll of remembrance was written in his presence concerning those who feared the Lord and honoured his name* (Malachi 3:16).

Astrology and Mediums

There are psychics, people who aspire to tell you of your past, and attempt to tell your future. Folk go to them desiring to know what is ahead of them. Deceived by what they are told they unconsciously try to fulfil the false prophecy themselves but only God knows the end from the beginning.

Others claim to hear from the dead and this can come through demonic deception. Desperate people longing to hear from their deceased loved ones go on believing what they hear despite the danger. Do not believe those who tell you they can contact the dead. This is what God has to say about contacting the dead:

> *When men tell you to consult mediums and spiritists, who whisper and mutter, should not a people inquire of their God? Why consult the dead on behalf of the living? To the law and to the testimony! If they do not speak according to this word, they have no light of dawn* (Isaiah 8:19-20).

What is God's opinion of those who read the stars and claim to discover the future through astrology? His opinion is full of sarcasm and through his prophet Isaiah he scorns those who try to govern their lives by believing lies!

> *Keep on, then, with your magic spells and with your many sorceries, which you have laboured at since childhood. Perhaps you will succeed, perhaps you will cause terror. All the counsel you have received has only worn you out! Let*

> *your astrologers come forward, those stargazers who make predictions month by month, let them save you from what is coming upon you. Surely they are like stubble; the fire will burn them up. They cannot even save themselves from the power of the flame. Here are no coals to warm anyone; here is no fire to sit by. That is all they can do for you – these you have laboured with and trafficked with since childhood. Each of them goes on in his error; there is no one that can save you* (Isaiah 47; 12-15)

God's opinion of those who claimed to be prophets of other gods and of their ability to predict the future was also very low –

> *'Present your case', says the Lord. 'Set forth your arguments', says Jacob's King. 'Bring in your idols, to tell us what is going to happen. Tell us what the former things were, so that we may consider them and know their final outcome. Or declare to us the things to come, tell us what the future holds, so we may know that you are gods. Do something, whether good or bad, so that we will be dismayed and filled with fear. But you are less than nothing and your works are utterly worthless; he who chooses you is detestable'* (41:21-24).

> *This is what the Lord says – Israel's King and Redeemer, the Lord Almighty; 'I am the first and I am the last; apart from me there is no God. Who then is like me? Let him proclaim it. Let him declare and lay out before me what has happened since I established my ancient people, and what is yet to come – yes, let him foretell what will come. Do not tremble, do not be afraid. Did I not proclaim this and foretell it long ago? You are my witnesses. Is there any God besides me? No, there is no other Rock; I know not one'* (44:6-8).

Consider These Things

There have been many attempts by mathematicians to work out the enormous odds of all the Old Testament prophecies concerning Jesus coming true in one man. Some have calculated that for all the prophecies to have been completed in one man's life amounts to 1 in 84 to the tenth power.[9] This would be an impossible task for any human but not impossible for God who knows the end from the beginning.

Take the twenty prophecies concerning the twenty-four hours encompassing the death of Christ which we list in chapter three of this book. These were given over centuries of time before the actual facts came to pass. For these to be fulfilled in one man, within one twenty-four hour period, is a miracle indeed.

Some may say that Christ knew scripture and was able to make sure that his life fulfilled scripture. This may be true in some things over which he had power, but what of all the other prophecies over which he had no control, such as his birth and his death!

Prophetic Paradoxes

Some of the Old Testament prophecies are called 'prophetic paradoxes'. On the surface they seem strange and puzzling, and the wise men of Jesus' day must have deemed it impossible that they could ever come to pass. These apparent paradoxes would always have remained a mystery if Christ had not come in the flesh, but then the prophecies became easy to reconcile as they miraculously revealed the wisdom of God. Here are some of them:

The first paradox was that Jesus was to be born in Bethlehem, brought out of Egypt, and also called a Nazarene. The following scriptures list these seemingly disparate prophecies which, as time proved, all fitted in beautifully as God arranged for Jesus to be born in Bethlehem, spend time in Egypt because of Herod's murderous decree, and then grow up in Nazareth.

He was to be born in Bethlehem. *But you Bethlehem Ephrathah, though you are small among the clans of Judah, out of you will*

---

[9] *Ibid.*

Another set of calculations can be found in the book by Stoner, Peter & Newman, Robert C. *Science Speaks*; Moody Press; Chicago Ill.; 1976. Pg. 104

come for me one who will be ruler over Israel, whose origins are from old, from ancient times (Micah 5:2).

And the New Testament fulfilment *Jesus was born in Bethlehem in Judea* (Matthew 2:1a).

He was to be brought out of Egypt. *When Israel was a child, I loved him, and out of Egypt I called my son* (Hosea 11:1).

Matthew saw the link here. *Out of Egypt I called my son* (Matthew 2:15b).

He was to be called a Nazarene. *A shoot (sprout) will come up from the stump of Jesse* (Isaiah 11:1).

Matthew once again saw the fulfilment *He shall be called a Nazarene* (Matthew 2:23b).[10]

A Nazarene referred to one who lived in Nazareth, which Jesus did. A Nazarite on the other hand was one who lived in the desert and lived the life of an ascetic. Possibly John the Baptist was a Nazarite, as he lived in the desert, dressed in camel's hair and ate locusts and wild honey (Matthew 3:4).

Similar paradoxes can be found throughout scripture –

Jesus was Father of eternity yet the Son of God during his time on earth.

> *For to us a child is born, to us a son is given, and the government will be upon his shoulders. And he will be called Wonderful Counsellor, Mighty God, Everlasting Father, Prince of Peace. Of the increase of his government and peace there will be no end. He will reign on David's throne and over his kingdom, establishing and upholding it with*

---

[10] *The Interpreter's Bible.* Volume 7; Abingdon Press; Nashville; Reference: Matthew 2:23: Pg. 262. Matthew apparently plays on words as the rabbis loved to do, and his point is: 'The scripture should be understood as saying *nocri* (Nazarene), not *nazir (*Nazarite) or *necer* (sprout).'

justice and righteousness from that time on and forever. The zeal of the Lord Almighty will accomplish this (Isaiah 9:6-7).

He was chosen by God yet despised by the Romans and Jews of his time.

The people stood watching, and the rulers even sneered at him. They said, 'He saved others; let him save himself if he is the Christ of God, the Chosen One' (Luke 23:35).

He was born King of the Jews, yet condemned and rejected by the crowd.

But they shouted, 'Take him away! Take him away! Crucify him' (John 19:15a).

He was born of a virgin with no earthly father.

But after he had considered this, an angel of the Lord appeared to him in a dream and said, 'Joseph, son of David, do not be afraid to take Mary home as your wife, because what is conceived in her is from the Holy Spirit. She will give birth to a son, and you are to give him the name Jesus, because he will save his people from their sins ... When Joseph woke up he did what the angel of the Lord had commanded him and took Mary home as his wife. But he had no union with her until she gave birth to a son. And he gave him the name Jesus (Matthew 1:20-21 & 24-25).

He was David's son yet he was David's Lord.

I will proclaim the decree of the Lord: He said to me, 'You are my Son; today I have become your Father. Ask of me, and I will make the nations your inheritance, the ends of the earth your possession. You will rule them with an iron sceptre; you will dash them to pieces like pottery' Therefore, you kings, be wise; be warned you rulers of the earth. Serve the Lord with fear and rejoice with trembling. Kiss the Son, lest he be angry and you be destroyed in your way, for his wrath can flare up in a moment. Blessed are all who take refuge in him (Psalm 2:7-12: cp. Matthew 22:41-45).

He was the Capstone yet also a rock of offense.

The stone the builders rejected has become the capstone; the Lord has done this, and it is marvellous in our eyes (Psalm 118:22-23; cp. Acts 4:8-12).

He pleased God in every way yet was hated by his own nation.

Those who passed by hurled insults at him, shaking their heads and saying, 'You who are going to destroy the temple and build it in three days, save yourself! Come down from the cross, if you are the Son of God!' In the same way the chief priests, the teachers of the law, and the elders mocked him. 'He saved others,' they said, 'but he can't save himself! He's the King of Israel! Let him come down from the cross, and we will believe in him.' (Matthew27:39-42).

He was without price yet sold for a mere thirty pieces of silver.

Come, all you who are thirsty, come to the waters; and you who have no money, come, buy and eat! Come, buy wine and milk without money and without cost (Isaiah 55:1; see also Matthew 26:14-16; 27:3-4).

He was not only rejected by men but forsaken by God on the cross.

From the sixth hour until the ninth hour darkness came over all the land. About the ninth hour Jesus cried out in a loud voice, 'Eloi, Eloi, lama sabachthani?' – which means, 'My God, my God, why have you forsaken me?' (Matthew 27:45-46).

He was pierced in his side yet not a bone of his body was broken.

But when they came to Jesus and found that he was already dead, they did not break his legs. Instead, one of the soldiers pierced Jesus' side with a spear, bringing a sudden flow of blood and water (John 19:33-34; Psalm 34:20).

He died as a guilt offering yet his days are prolonged.

Therefore my heart is glad and my tongue rejoices; my body also will rest secure, because you will not abandon me to the grave, nor will you let your Holy One see decay (Psalm 16:9-10).

He is now High Priest yet also a king enthroned.

Jesus, who went before us, has entered on our behalf. He has become a high priest forever, in the order of Melchizedek. This Melchizedek was king of Salem and priest of God Most High (Hebrews 6:19-20).

Even though before Jesus came these statements were all seemingly impossible of total fulfilment, yet they worked out easily in the life of Jesus Christ our Saviour and Lord.

40

Chapter Three:

Prophetic Details

Prophecies Concerning His Birth

He would crush Satan (Genesis 3:15). Right at the beginning, before Adam and Eve were cast out of the Garden of Eden, God promised one would come to crush the head of the serpent and put things right for the human race. However, in the struggle the offspring of the woman would be wounded in his heel. That hurt was not specified in detail at the time but we know now that it was an early intimation of the fact that Jesus, the one who was to come, would crush Satan's power but in the process would be nailed to a cross.

He would be born of a virgin (Isaiah 7:14). Here again is a prophecy with two fulfilments. Isaiah gives a prophecy concerning a child to be born. He begins with the present but gives the prophecy a Messianic fulfilment also.

John D. Watts in his commentary on Isaiah states –

> A young woman who is apparently present or contemporary, but not yet married (i.e. a virgin) will in due course bear a child and call his name Immanuel, meaning *'God-is-With-Us.'* By the time the child is old enough to make decisions, the land of the two opposing kings will be devastated.[11]

This prophecy was recalled by Matthew as he realised the Messianic significance of it in Matthew 1:22-23 –

> *All this took place to fulfil what the Lord had said through the prophet. 'The virgin will be with child and will give birth*

---

[11] Watts, John D. *World Biblical Commentary* (Isaiah 1-33); Word Books; 1985

to a son, and they will call him Immanuel – which means, 'God with us'.

His Birthplace

The place of his birth is described (Micah 5:2). As we have seen the Messiah was to be born in Bethlehem. It was here the Moabitess Ruth settled with her husband Boaz and here their son, Obed, was born (Ruth 4:13-22). His son, Jesse, in turn was father to David and in this vicinity David shepherded his father's sheep (1 Samuel 17:12). Bethlehem was the town of David, which explains why Joseph and Mary, who were of the line of David, had to journey there for the census (Luke 2:4). Here we see the overruling hand of God as the Roman Caesar made the decision for this particular census in precise time for Jesus to be born in Bethlehem.

His Birth Announced

The angel Gabriel declared to Mary that she would have a son through the overshadowing of the Holy Spirit. She was to call his name Jesus for he would save his people from their sins (Luke 1:26-35).

A great company of the angels of God also heralded his birth and told the shepherds where they could find him to worship him (2:8-20).

The Magi, the wise men from the east, declared his birth and followed the wonderful star to Bethlehem (Matthew 2:1-12).

His Birth Confirmed

Simeon was waiting to welcome Mary and Joseph on the day they brought Jesus into the temple to offer the required sacrifice of two doves and to have his birth recorded. Luke tell us of this momentous day –

> *Now there was a man in Jerusalem called Simeon, who was righteous and devout. He was waiting for the consolation of*

> *Israel, and the Holy Spirit was upon him. It had been revealed to him by the Holy Spirit that he would not die before he had seen the Lord's Christ. Moved by the Spirit, he went into the temple courts. When the parents brought in the child Jesus to do for him what the custom of the Law required, Simeon took him in his arms and praised God saying: 'Sovereign Lord as you have promised, you now dismiss your servant in peace. For my eyes have seen your salvation, which you have prepared in the sight of all people, a light for revelation to the Gentiles and for glory to your people Israel'* (Luke 2:25-32).

Anna the prophetess, who was eighty four years of age and the daughter of Phanuel, had lived in the temple after her widowhood for more than sixty years and had spent her time in fasting and prayer. She came forward also to bless the baby Jesus and give thanks to God for the redemption of Israel (2:36-38).

The Forerunner of His Birth

The fore-runner of his birth is predicted in Malachi–

> *'See, I will send my messenger, who will prepare the way before me. Then suddenly the Lord you are seeking will come to his temple; the messenger of the covenant, whom you desire, will come', says the Lord Almighty* (Malachi 3:1-2)
> *'See, I will send you the prophet Elijah before that great and dreadful day of the Lord comes'* (Malachi 4:5)

In Luke (1:17) the angel Gabriel told Zechariah in the temple that his promised son, who was to be named John, would fulfil the prophecy of Malachi, and Jesus confirmed that John the Baptist was the Elijah who was to come and prepare the way for him (Matthew 17:10-13).

The Purpose Of His Birth

The purpose of his birth is declared in Isaiah –

> *But he was pierced for our transgressions, he was crushed for our iniquities; the punishment that brought us peace was upon him, and by his wounds we are healed* (Isaiah 53:5).

An interesting insight taken from a study by Arthur E. Glass draws attention to the name of Jesus hidden in the Old Testament one hundred times, from Genesis to Habakkuk:

> Every time the Old Testament uses the word SALVATION (especially with the Hebrew suffix meaning 'my', 'thy' or 'his,' with very few exceptions (when the word is used in an impersonal sense) it is identically the same word as YESHUA (Jesus). This is actually what the angel said to Joseph in Matthew 1:21 – *'Thou shalt call his name YESHUA (salvation)'* One example we find in Psalm 9:13b-14, *'Have mercy and lift me up from the gates of death, that I may declare your praises in the gates of the daughter of Zion and there rejoice in your Yeshua' (salvation).*[12]

His Public Ministry Foretold

Even the timing of his ministry was given to Daniel the prophet.

Daniel was praying to God, confessing the sin of Israel and pleading with the Lord to remember he had prophesied through Jeremiah that the children of Israel would return to their land after seventy years in captivity (Jeremiah 25:11; 29:10-14). The seventy years were almost up and Daniel was reminding the Lord of his promise. While he was praying an angel came to him and told him the things that were to come (Daniel 9:20-26a). **The prophecy concerning the Messiah gives the exact year he would appear in his temple –**

---

[12] From a pamphlet; *Yeshua in the Tenach*, by Arthur Glass circa 1945; quoted in Lockyer's; *All the Messianic Prophecies of the Bible;* Zondervan Publishing; 1960. Pg. 66.

> *From the issuing of the decree to restore and rebuild Jerusalem until the Anointed One, the Ruler comes there will be seven sevens, and sixty-two sevens* (483 years). *After the sixty-two sevens the Anointed one will be cut off and will have nothing* (Daniel 9:25-26a).

So we see that 483 years from the time of Daniel's prophecy Jesus, the Messiah, came to his temple in Jerusalem. This momentous occasion was foretold by Daniel nearly 500 years before it occurred.

> This 483 years is the time between the decree to rebuild Jerusalem and the coming of the 'Anointed One' (Daniel 9:25). The decree to rebuild Jerusalem... was 457 B.C. Adding 483 years to 457 B.C. we arrive at A.D. 26 the year that Jesus was baptised and began his ministry. A most remarkable fulfilment of Daniel's prophecy, even to the year.
>
> Further, within 3 1/2 years Jesus was crucified, that is, in the midst of the one week 'the Anointed one' was 'cut off', 'purged away sin and brought in everlasting righteousness' (Daniel 9: 24, 26, 27).[13]

Daniel also prophesied that Jesus would be killed before the destruction of the temple (Daniel 9:26), and Jesus himself predicted its destruction (Matthew 24:1-3).

Note: For those puzzled by the fact that Jesus was thirty years of age in 26 A.D. instead of 30 A.D. The year of Jesus birth was given very accurately by Luke in chapter two of his gospel. Joseph and Mary had to go to Bethlehem where Jesus was born for the first census after Quirinius became governor of Syria (Luke 2:1-2) which occurred around 5 B.C. [14]

---

[13] Halley, Henry H. *Halley's Bible Handbook*; Zondervan Publishing; Grand Rapids, Michigan; 1976. Pg.349

[14] Zondervan's *Pictorial Encyclopedia of the Bible;* Reference 'Quirinius'. Pgs. 5&6. (His) intervention could easily have postponed the actual date of registration

This being the case then Jesus would have been around thirty years of age in 26 A.D.

His Healing Ministry Foreshadowed

His ministry would be a healing, restoring ministry and he would bring a new covenant to his people –

> *I, the Lord, have called you in righteousness; I will take hold of your hand, I will keep you and make you to be a covenant for the people and a light for the Gentiles, to open eyes that are blind, to free captives from prison and to release from the dungeon those who sit in darkness* (Isaiah 42:6-7; also 61:1-3).

He Would Preach in Galilee

Almost all his disciples came from Galilee. Here the people heard Jesus gladly for they had been labouring under the burden of all the nit-picking laws laid on them by the Pharisees. There were extra laws against reaping, threshing, winnowing, and preparing food. For instance a woman could not pull out a grey hair from her head without being accused of reaping!

> *Nevertheless there will be no more gloom for those who were in distress. In the past he humbled the land of Zebulun and the land of Naphtali, but in the future he will honour Galilee of the Gentiles, by the way of the sea, along the Jordan – The people walking in darkness have seen a great light; on those living in the land of the shadow of death a light has dawned* (Isaiah 9:1-2).

---

to the end of 5 B.C. a reasonable date. (The matter is argued at length in Appendix Four of *The Century of the New Testament* by E. M. Blaiklock).

His Character Revealed in Scripture

Here is a list of the aspects of the character of Christ in his humanity, revealing both the Old Testament prophecy and the New Testament fulfilment of each character trait Jesus was –

Courageous and Strong: Jesus must have seen many die horribly on a cross during the first thirty years of his life on earth and yet, knowing this was to be his fate, he did not falter from the pathway that he had agreed to walk.

> *Who is this coming from Edom, from Bosrah, with his garments stained crimson? Who is this robed in splendour, striding forward in the greatness of his strength? 'It is I, speaking in righteousness, mighty to save ... I looked, but there was no one to help, I was appalled that no one gave support; so my own arm worked salvation for me, and my own wrath sustained me'* (Isaiah 63:1&5).

> *From that time on Jesus began to explain to his disciples that he must go to Jerusalem and suffer many things at the hands of the elders, chief priests and teachers of the law, and that he must be killed and on the third day be raised to life* (Matthew 16:21).

Compassionate: Jesus was often moved with compassion by the plight of the sick and suffering. As soon as he ascertained the faith of the individual he was ready to say, *'Your faith has healed you'*, as he did to the woman with the issue of blood (Matthew 9:22).

> *The Spirit of the Sovereign Lord is on me, because the Lord has anointed me to preach good news to the poor. He has sent me to bind up the broken hearted, to proclaim freedom for the captives, and release from darkness for the prisoners* (Isaiah 61:1).

> *When he saw the crowds, he had compassion on them, because they were harassed and helpless, like sheep without a shepherd* (Matthew 9:36).

Faithful: Jesus was faithful to his calling and completed all that he had been born to fulfil, he finished the work God had given him to do. God's will was his will (John 19:30).

> *Righteousness will be his belt and faithfulness the sash around his waist* (Isaiah 11:5)
>
> *If we are faithless, he will remain faithful, for he cannot disown himself* (2 Timothy 2:13).

Forgiving: Jesus' solemn warning comes to us through the parable of the merciless servant (Matthew 18:21-35). We must forgive as he forgives (Mark 11:25).

> *You are forgiving and good, O Lord, abounding in love to all who call on you* (Psalm 86:5).
>
> *Jesus said, 'Father forgive them, for they do not know what they are doing'* (Luke 23:34).

Good: Because of his goodness death could not hold Jesus. He was without sin and he was declared to be the powerful Son of God by his resurrection from the dead (Romans 1:1-4).

> *Good and upright is the Lord; therefore he instructs sinners in his ways. He guides the humble in what is right and teaches them his way* (Psalm 25:8-9).
>
> *Like newborn babies, crave pure spiritual milk, so that by it you may grow up in your salvation, now that you have tasted that the Lord is good* (1 Peter 2:2-3).

Innocent, Pure and Holy: Jesus was holy, he was born holy (Luke 1:35), he lived a holy life, even the demons knew he was holy (Mark 1:24). Now he reigns in awesome majesty in the glory of heaven (Exodus 15:11).

> *I wash my hands in innocence, and go about your altar, O Lord, proclaiming aloud your praise and telling of all your wonderful deeds (*Psalm 26:6-7).
>
> *Can any of you prove me guilty of sin?* (John 8:46a).

Just: Jesus is to be our righteous judge and we who long for his appearing will receive a crown of righteousness (2 Timothy 4:8).

> *Of the increase of his government and peace there will be no end. He will reign on David's throne and over his kingdom, establishing and upholding it with justice and righteousness from that time on and forever. The zeal of the Lord Almighty will accomplish this* (Isaiah 9:7)

> *By myself I can do nothing; I judge only as I hear, and my judgment is just, for I seek not to please myself but him who sent me* (John 5:30).

Love: John, the disciple who was the closest to the Lord Jesus, tells us in his first letter that God's love, through Christ, has been lavished upon us, so much so that we too are to be called God's children (1 John 3:1).

> *The Lord appeared to us in the past saying, 'I have loved you with an everlasting love; I have drawn you with loving kindness* (Jeremiah 31:3).

> *Greater love has no one than this, that he lay down his life for his friends* (John 15:13).

Meek: Jesus was meek but he was never weak; he knew who he was and in that strength he accomplished all he was sent to do and finished the work he was born to complete.

> *He was oppressed and afflicted, yet he did not open his mouth; he was led like a lamb to the slaughter, and as a sheep before her shearers is silent, so he did not open his mouth* (Isaiah 53:7).

> *Take my yoke upon you and learn from me, for I am gentle and humble in heart, and you will find rest for your soul. For my yoke is easy and my burden is light* (Matthew 11:29-30).

Merciful: Jesus had pity on his people in their sickness and sorrow, he feels with us today as he did then and is a friend who sticks closer than a brother (Proverbs 18:24; Matthew 28:20b).

> *But in your great mercy you did not put an end to them nor abandon them, for you are a gracious and merciful God* (Nehemiah 9:31).
>
> *As Jesus was getting into the boat, the man who had been demon-possessed begged to go with him. Jesus did not let him, but said, 'Go home to your family and tell them how much the Lord has done for you, and how he has had mercy on you* (Mark 5:18-19).

Obedient: Jesus was always obedient to his Father. He said he could do nothing of himself but only the things he saw his Father doing (John 5:19).

> *Then I said, 'Here I am, I have come- it is written about me in the scroll. I desire to do your will, O my God; your law is within my heart'* (Psalm 40:7-8).
>
> *And being found in appearance as a man, he humbled himself and became obedient to death, – even death on a cross* (Philippians 2:8).

Patient: Jesus suffered patiently his degradation at the hands of the creatures he had created. How longsuffering he was under extreme provocation.

> *He was oppressed and afflicted, yet he did not open his mouth; he was led like a lamb to the slaughter, and as a sheep before her shearers is silent, so he did not open his mouth* (Isaiah 53:7).
>
> *Then the governor's soldiers took Jesus into the Praetorium and gathered the whole company of soldiers around him. They stripped him and put a scarlet robe on him, and then twisted together a crown of thorns and set it on his head. They put a staff in his right hand and knelt in front of him and mocked him. 'Hail, king of the Jews!' they said, They spit on him, and took the staff and struck him on the head again and again. After they had mocked him, they took off*

the robe and put his own clothes on him. Then they led him away to crucify him (Matthew 27:27-31).

Righteous: Jesus had no sin in him; therefore he was righteous before God.

After the suffering of his soul, he will see the light of life and be satisfied; by his knowledge my righteous servant will justify many, and he will bear their iniquities (Isaiah 53:11).

You have loved righteousness and hated wickedness; therefore God, your God, has set you above your companions by anointing you with the oil of joy (Hebrews 1:9).

Steadfast: Jesus set himself to fulfil his Father's will, no matter what it cost him.

Because the Sovereign Lord helps me, I will not be disgraced. Therefore have I set my face like a flint, and I know I will not be put to shame (Isaiah 50:7).

We are going up to Jerusalem, and the Son of Man will be betrayed to the chief priests and the teachers of the law. They will condemn him to death and will turn him over to the Gentiles to be mocked and flogged and crucified. On the third day he will be raised to life! (Matthew 20:18-19)

Truthful and full of Integrity: Jesus is the way the truth and the life (John 14:6), no one comes to the Father except through him.

All your words are true; all your righteous laws are eternal (Psalm 119:160).

'Teacher,' they said, 'we know you are a man of integrity and that you teach the way of God in accordance with the truth. You aren't swayed by men, because you pay no attention to who they are' (Matthew 22:16b).

Wise: Jesus had all the wisdom of his Father. Jesus was wise in his answering of the probing questions of the scribes and Pharisees. He was never at a loss and answered them in such a way that it left them speechless and discomfited. There is one instance in Matthew 21:23-27, and there is another in Mark –

> *'Great is our Lord and mighty in power; his understanding has no limit'* (Psalm 147:5).

> *Later they sent some of the Pharisees and Herodians to Jesus to catch him in his words...Should we pay (taxes) or shouldn't we? But Jesus knew their hypocrisy. 'Why are you trying to trap me?' he asked. 'Bring me a denarius and let me look at it.' They brought him the coin, and he asked them, 'Whose portrait is this? And whose inscription'? 'Caesar's', they replied. Then Jesus said to them, 'Give to Caesar what is Caesar's and to God what is God's.' And they were amazed at him* (Mark 12:13a,15-17).

Zealous: Jesus was zealous for his Father's house and drove the money changers out of the temple with a whip (John 2:13-16).

> *He put on righteousness as his breastplate, and the helmet of salvation on his head: he put on the garments of vengeance and wrapped himself in zeal as in a cloak* (Isaiah 59:17).

> *When it was almost time for the Jewish Passover, Jesus went up to Jerusalem. In the temple courts he found men selling cattle, sheep and doves, and others sitting at tables exchanging money. So he made a whip out of cords, and drove all from the temple area, both sheep and cattle; he scattered the coins of the money changers and overturned their tables. To those who sold doves he said, 'Get these out of here! How dare you turn my Father's house into a market!' His disciples remembered that it is written: 'Zeal for your house will consume me'* (John 2:13-17).

He Was Both God and Man

His deity: Jesus was not a pseudo man, nor was he a phantom, as the Gnostics would have us believe. He was a real man yet within himself he also held his eternal Godhead veiled from human eyes, except for the transcending experience on Mt Tabor (Luke 9:28-36).

> *The Lord says to my Lord: 'Sit at my right hand until I make your enemies a footstool for your feet'* (Psalm 110:1).

> *Philip said, 'Lord, show us the Father and that will be enough for us.' Jesus answered, 'Don't you know me, Philip, even after I have been among you such a long time? Anyone who has seen me has seen the Father'* (John 14:8-9a).

His humanity: Jesus lived here on earth, he worked hard as a carpenter (Luke 2:51), he blessed the little children (Luke 18:15-17), he grew weary at times (John 4:6), he had compassion on the sick (Matthew 9:36), and he wept in sympathy with his friends when Lazarus died even though he knew he would live again (John 11:35), and finally he made the ultimate sacrifice, suffering and dying to rescue all who believe (John 3:16).

> *'But I am a worm and not a man, scorned by men and despised by the people'* (Psalm 22:6).

> *Jesus replied, 'Foxes have holes and birds of the air have nests, but the Son of Man has nowhere to lay his head'* (Luke 9:58).

His Triumphant Entry into Jerusalem Foretold

There was a tradition in Old Testament days that if a conqueror rode into a city on a horse he was declaring war on the inhabitants, but if he rode into the city on a donkey then he came in peace. Jesus rode into Jerusalem on a donkey's colt that had never been ridden before (Luke 19:30-35) showing his perfect control over all earthly creatures. He came to his own in peace but, though the common people who loved him shouted hosannas (Luke 19:38), many of the Pharisees and the teachers of the law did not receive him (19:47). They later rose up in hatred and put him to death on a cross.

Rejoice greatly, O daughter of Zion! Shout, daughter of Jerusalem! See, your king comes to you, righteous and having salvation, gentle and riding on a donkey, on a colt, the foal of a donkey (Zechariah 9:9 and see also Matthew 21:1-11).

His Death Accurately Predicted

The twenty prophecies listed below were all fulfilled in the life of Jesus within a twenty four hour period and they show the exact foreknowledge of God.

The Jews and Gentiles would combine against him

This was prophesied B.C.1000 (Psalm 2:1-2) and fulfilled when the Jewish priests and the Romans together brought about Jesus' death (Matthew 27:20-24; Acts 4:27).

He would be betrayed by a friend

This was prophesied B.C. 1000 (Psalm 41:9) and fulfilled when Judas betrayed Jesus to the priests (Luke 22:47-48; John 13:18-30; 18:1-7).

He was to be forsaken by his disciples

This was prophesied B.C. 487 (Zechariah 13:7b) and fulfilled when his disciples fled on the eve of Jesus' arrest (Matthew 26:56b).

He was to be sold for 30 pieces of silver

This was prophesied B.C. 487 (Zechariah 11:12) and fulfilled when Judas accepted the money to betray Jesus (Matthew 26:14-16).

He was to be smitten

This was prophesied B.C. 710 (Micah 5:1b) and fulfilled when the Roman soldiers tormented Jesus (Matthew 27:30).

He was to be spit upon and scourged

This was prophesied B.C. 712 (Isaiah 50:6) and fulfilled when some of the members of the Sanhedrin spat on Jesus and struck him with their fists, and then when the Roman soldiers flogged him and spat on him (Mark 14:65; Matthew 27:26-31; John 19:1-3).

He was to be nailed to a cross

This was prophesied B.C. 1000 (Psalm 22:16) and fulfilled when Jesus was nailed to the cross by the Roman soldiers (John 19:16-18).

He was to be forsaken by God

This was prophesied B.C. 1000 (Psalm 22:1) and fulfilled when Jesus cried out upon the cross, '*My God, my God, why have you forsaken me?*' Matthew 27:46b).

He was to be mocked

This was prophesied B.C. 1000 (Psalm 22:7-8) and fulfilled when Jesus was mocked by those passing by the cross (Matthew 27:39-44).

He was to have gall and vinegar given him to drink

This was prophesied B.C. 1000 (Psalm 69:21) and fulfilled when Jesus was offered wine mixed with gall, though he refused to drink it (Matthew 27:34).

His suffering was to be intense

This was prophesied B.C. 1000 (Psalm 22:14-15) and fulfilled in the garden of Gethsemane where Jesus prayed about his coming trial so earnestly that his perspiration was like great drops of blood and he had to be strengthened by an angel, and later as he agonised on the cross (Matthew 27:45-46; Luke 22:42-44).

He was to suffer for others

This was prophesied B.C. 712 (Isaiah 53:4-6) and fulfilled as Jesus did not suffer for himself because he was sinless. He died for us who are born in sin (Matthew 20:28).

He was to be patient and silent under suffering

This was prophesied B.C. 710 (Isaiah 53:7) and fulfilled because Jesus was silent before Herod and before the Roman soldiers who tormented him (Luke 23:8; Matthew 27:12-14).

His garments were to be divided and gambled over

This was prophesied B.C. 1000 (Psalm 22:18) and fulfilled when the Roman soldiers cast lots for Jesus' clothing (Matthew 27:35).

He was to be numbered with the transgressors

This was prophesied B.C. 712 (Isaiah 53:12) and fulfilled when Jesus was crucified between two thieves (Mark 15:27; Matthew 27:38).

He was to intercede for his murderers

This was prophesied B.C. 712 (Isaiah 53:12b) and fulfilled when Jesus prayed for his murderers, *'Father forgive them, for they do not know what they are doing'* (Luke 23:34).

He was to die

This was prophesied B.C. 712 (Isaiah 53:12) and fulfilled when Jesus voluntarily gave up his spirit. As he told his disciples, *'I have authority to lay (my life) down and authority to take it up again. This command I received from my Father'* (John 10:17-18; Matthew 27:50).

Not a bone of his body was to be broken

This was prophesied B.C. 1491 (Exodus 12:46) and again B.C. 1000 (Psalm 34:20), and was fulfilled when the soldiers came to break Jesus' legs to hasten his death. Instead, having discovered

Jesus was already dead, one pierced his side with a spear (John 19:33- 36).

He was to be pierced

This was prophesied B.C. 487 (Zechariah 12:10) and fulfilled when Jesus' side was pierced and blood and water gushed out (John 19:34-37).

He was to be buried with the rich

This was prophesied B.C. 712 (Isaiah 53:9) and fulfilled when the rich Joseph of Arimathea asked to bury Jesus in the grave he had prepared for himself (Matthew 27:57-60).

More Prophecies Concerning Jesus –

His flesh would not be corrupted

This was prophesied B.C. 1000 (Psalm 16:9-10) and fulfilled when Jesus was raised on the third day (Matthew 28:1-6; Acts 2:29-36).

He was to be resurrected

This was prophesied B.C. 1000 (Psalm 16:10) and discovered when the women went to the tomb with the embalming spices and found the stone rolled away. Two angels then reminded them of Jesus' prophecy concerning his death and resurrection Luke 24:1-8).

He was to ascend on high

This was prophesied B.C. 1000 (Psalm 68:18) and fulfilled as Jesus told his disciples before his ascension, *'All authority in heaven and on earth has been given to me'* (Matthew 28:18; Luke 24:50-53; see also Ephesians 4:7-10).

He was to sit on the right hand of God

This was prophesied B.C. 1000 (Psalm 110:1) and confirmed as being fulfilled in Hebrews 1:3b which was written in A.D. 60.

Jesus' Ministry was Predicted by the Prophets

He was to be a Prophet according to Moses -

The Lord said to me: 'What they say is good. I will raise up for them a prophet like you from among their brothers, I will put my words in his mouth, and he will tell them everything I command him. (Deuteronomy 17-18)

As Stephen confirmed in his rousing and anointed sermon before the Sanhedrin (Acts 7:37) Jesus fulfilled the office of prophet. He foretold many things during his ministry. Some have already come to pass and others are still to be fulfilled. He predicted his own death and resurrection (Matthew 20:18-19), the destruction of the temple (Matthew 24:1-2), and the end of all things (24:4-51).

Jesus was to be a Priest –

The Lord has sworn and will not change his mind; 'You are a priest forever, in the order of Melchizedek' (Psalm 110:4).

Now Jesus is our High Priest in the order of Melchizedek and not in the order of Aaron. The priesthood of Jesus is based on the power of an indestructible life. Death could not hold the Son of God (Hebrews 7:11-22), and his priesthood will never end –

Because Jesus lives forever, he has a permanent priesthood. Therefore he is able to save completely those who come to God through him, because he always lives to intercede for them (verses 24-25).

Jesus was to be a King above all other kings and this also was prophesied in Psalm 2 and Psalm 24 –

I will proclaim the decree of the Lord. He said to me, 'You are my Son; today I have become your Father. Ask of me, and I will make the nations your inheritance, the ends of the earth your possession. You will rule them with an iron sceptre: you will dash them to pieces like pottery' (Psalm 2:7-9).

> *Lift up your heads, O you gates; lift them up, you ancient doors, that the King of glory may come in. Who is he, this King of glory? The Lord Almighty –he is the King of glory* (Psalm 24:9-10).

Jesus was to be King of kings, he is far above all things in heaven and on earth, visible and invisible, thrones and powers, rulers and authorities. He is before all things and in him all things hold together as Paul tells us in Colossians and again in his letter to Timothy–

> *God, the blessed and only Ruler, the King of kings and Lord of lords, who alone is immortal and who lives in unapproachable light, whom no one has seen or can see. To him be honour and might forever. Amen* (1 Timothy 6:15b-16; see also Revelation 19:11-16).

Jesus was to be an Advocate; an Intercessor, one who intercedes for the people.

> *Even now my witness is in heaven, my advocate is on high. My intercessor is my friend as my eyes pour out tears to God; on behalf of a man he pleads with God as a man pleads for his friend* (Job 16:19-21).

Right now Jesus is interceding for us. He understands and he sympathises with our weaknesses because he too was tempted in every way, but he remained sinless, without spot or blemish. Because of his perfect life we can come before the Father without fear, perfectly confident that he will hear our prayers and grant us the mercy and grace we need in our daily life (Hebrews 4:14-16). Jesus is our perfect advocate –

> *Therefore he is able to save completely those who come to God through him, because he always lives to intercede for them* (Hebrews 7:25).

Jesus was to be a Guarantor, one who warrants that he will pay another's debt. Jesus has not only promised to be our Guarantor, he has paid our debt in full so that we can be free from our sin.

The Lord works righteousness and justice for all the oppressed (Psalm 103:6).

Because of this oath, Jesus has become the guarantee of a better covenant (Hebrews 7:22).

Chapter Four:

The Fascination of Typology

The types and shadows of the Old Testament are indeed fascinating but we are warned to be very careful in our studies of these word pictures.

> Nothing may be dogmatically asserted to be a type without explicit New Testament authority. All types not so authenticated must be recognized as having the authority of analogy (likeness or similarity), or spiritual congruity (agreement or harmony) merely.[15]

Principles of Interpretation.

Scofield's assertion may be too strong, but certainly no doctrine or theory should be built upon a type or types independently of direct teaching elsewhere in scripture.. Types are meant to *amplify* doctrine, not to *originate* doctrine. They are types, not originals. **Types are dependent on the reality they represent.** The parallelism between type and anti-type should not be pressed to fanciful extremes. Types are not meant to be exact replicas.

Definition and Classification.

We find a careful definition of types in the wisdom of J. Sidlow Baxter.

> A type may be said to be any person, object, event, act or institution Divinely adapted to represent some spiritual reality, or to prefigure some person or truth to be later revealed. Or, to put it another way – God has been pleased to

---

[15] Scofield, C. I. *The Scofield Reference Bible*; Notes on Exodus 25:1; Oxford University Press; 1909.

invest certain persons, objects, events, acts, institutions, with a pre-figurative meaning, so that besides having a real relationship with their own times they have had a significance reaching far forward into the future.[16]

Bearing this definition in mind, types cannot and must not be forced to say what they manifestly do not say. For instance some parts of Abraham's life indicate a type of God the Father but at other times he is only too human, showing fear and deceiving others for his own safety. Keeping this in mind, types still remain fascinating to those Bible students who enjoy studying the Old Testament to find Jesus' life and ministry depicted through history, ritual and prophecy.

Some of the following types will be mentioned in the New Testament and thus verified, others will still be of interest, showing a likeness to the life and character of Christ. Those that are mentioned in the New Testament are to be taken seriously as they are inspired shadows of things to come. They were placed there by God's foreknowledge to teach us eternal truths and help us to understand his purposes. The Apostle Paul acknowledges this concerning the wilderness wanderings –

> *These things happened to them as examples and were written down as warnings for us, on whom the fulfilment of the ages has come* (1 Corinthians 10:11).

Other types (that is, those that are not directly cited by the apostles) still unfold many fascinating ideas but cannot hold the same divine authority.

Noah's Ark - A Type of Salvation.

God chose Noah to build an ark to save his family from the flood he was bringing on the earth (Genesis 6:8-9). He also planned the building of it to certain specifications as he knew how much room

---

[16] Baxter, J. Sidlow; *Explore the Book*; Volume One; Marshall, Morgan and Scott; Ltd. London 1951; Pg. 56

would be needed to house Noah's family and all of the chosen animals. It was to be built of cypress or gopher wood as this wood was greatly prized as the very best building material for fashioning boats. Pitch was used in all the joints, inside and outside, to make the ark water proof (Genesis 6:14-16)

The ark had only one entrance but it had a very high opening giving light and air *'Make a roof for it and finish the ark to within eighteen inches of the top'* (Genesis 6:16). Through this opening light would have penetrated into the whole structure,

There are many fascinating types we can draw from the ark.

The purpose of the ark was a safe place of refuge for Noah and his family from the flood waters. Jesus is our safe place of refuge in which we can shelter (Psalm 46:1; Hebrews 6:17-20; John 10:28; Ephesians 2:5-10).

The ark was a safe place for Noah's family but it was a sign of destruction for the rest of mankind (Genesis 7:22). When the gospel is accepted it is a source of eternal life to those who believe, but if it is rejected it brings judgment to both men and women (2 Corinthians 2:15-16; Hebrews 9:15).

The pitch protected Noah and his family from the waters of judgment and this word 'pitch' is the same word used for 'atonement'. It represents the blood of Jesus which makes atonement for our souls (Leviticus 17:11).

The ark had only one entrance, and when they were all inside God shut the door (Genesis 7:16b). Jesus spoke of himself as the door, the only way whereby we can enter the kingdom of God (John 10:1-9). One day God will close that door, time will end and judgment will begin. Then it will be too late for people to accept Christ as their Saviour (Matthew 25:10-13).

So the ark was a symbol of our Lord; of his salvation and our rescue, refuge and deliverance from the coming judgment.

Noah's Ark – A Type of The Church

Noah's family were chosen and party to a covenant (Genesis 6:18). Christian believers are also chosen and have a new covenant (2 Thessalonians 2:13; Ephesians 1:4). They were called (Genesis 7:1). We are also called (Romans 8:29-30; 1 Corinthians 1:9). They were believers; Noah believed God (Genesis 7:5-7) *'By faith Noah, when warned about things not yet seen, in holy fear built an ark to save his family* (Hebrews 11:7). Christians also believe by faith (Romans 10: 8-10; Hebrews 10:39).

Noah's faith made him obedient (Genesis 6:22; 7:5). Christians must also be obedient (1 Peter 1:22; Romans 16:25-27). Noah's faith was imputed to him for righteousness (Genesis 7:1; Hebrews 11:7). Christians have righteousness imputed to them (Romans 5:1; 10:4).

Noah and his family were separated; first by their lifestyle and then by the ark. Christians too are separated (John 17:16; 2 Corinthians 6:17; 1 Peter 2:9). Noah and his family were sealed into the ark (Genesis.7:16) *'Then the Lord shut him in'*. Christians too are sealed by the Holy Spirit of promise (Ephesians 1:13-14; 4:30; 2 Corinthians 1:21-22).

Noah's family rose above the judgment of the flood waters (Genesis 7:17-20). Christians are saved by the resurrection of Christ; as they judge themselves they will not have to be judged (1 Corinthians 11:23-32; 1 Peter 3:21; Colossians 3:1-4). Noah's family were rewarded, they survived and were put into possession of a new world (Genesis 8:15-19). Christians too will be rewarded (2 Peter 3:13; Revelation 21:1-4).

Jacob's Ladder – A Type of The Cross

Jacob fled from his father's house and the only family life he knew. Night came on, and he stopped to sleep. He had stolen his brother's blessing and his birthright through a trick, but he was also God's choice to continue the family line. God was in the process of reshaping him and eventually he would be changed from Jacob, the deceitful, to Israel, a prince with God. While he slept he dreamed (Genesis 28:10-15), and in his dream he saw a ladder resting on the earth and reaching up to heaven. On that ladder angels were ascending and descending. Above them stood the Lord, who restated the covenant he had made with Abraham, so that this covenant belonged also to Jacob! (Genesis 13:14-17).

The ladder seen by Jacob is a symbol of the cross which was to come and which bridges the vast gulf between God and mankind, Jesus our Saviour dying on that cross is our link between earth and heaven (John 1:51; 14:6; Acts 4:12).

The Miraculous Bush - A Symbol of Jesus.

When Moses saw the bush burning but not being consumed to ashes he went to see what this phenomenon could be (Exodus 3:2-22). The angel of the Lord spoke to Moses from the flames of the bush and revealed himself as a holy God, the God of his ancestors, Abraham, Isaac and Jacob. God gave to Moses the commission to go and free the people of Israel and in the process he revealed himself as the great I AM (Exodus 3:14; John 8:58).

The fire of God cannot be put out by the philosophies of men, they have all tried but none have succeeded. This bush that burned without being consumed was a symbol of Christ the great I AM (Revelation 1:12-18). Communism, Atheism, Humanism, Modernism, Materialism, and Post-Modernism are all useless chimeras, fated to fade into history when faced by the Might and the Power of the Son of God.

The church of Jesus Christ is also unconquerable, it cannot be defeated (Matthew 16:15-19). It may appear at times and in various places to be faltering, but when it dies in one place it rises with new vigour in another, and the more persecution it attracts the more it grows in purity and strength.

The Passover — The Sacrifice of Christ

When the children of Israel were given the solemn task of sprinkling the door of their house in Egypt with the blood of the sacrificial lamb they were saving their first-born from death and setting the stage for a memorial Passover Feast (Exodus 12:1-30). This feast of a lamb roasted with fire and eaten with unleavened bread and bitter herbs, was to be consumed by the Israelites with their cloaks tucked into their belts, sandals on their feet, and a staff in their hands; poised and ready for flight. As the children of Israel continued this ritual year after year it would be a memorial of their need for a sacrifice that was to come. This sacrifice of Christ, though not to occur until many years in the future, would satisfy the requirements of the judgment of God on sinful men and women forever.

We shelter under the blood of Christ and we eat the bread and drink the cup of the communion by faith confident that we are saved, healed, and forgiven by God (1 Corinthians 11:17-34). Eating the unleavened bread as a symbol of the body of Christ indicates a separation from all evil (1 Corinthians 5:7-8). Drinking the wine, or grape juice, as a symbol of the blood of Christ, reminds us that his blood cleanses us from all sin (1John 1:8-9).

In Egypt the blood of the spotless lamb was applied to the doorposts and the family inside were then safe from the angel of death. Not a bone of the body of the lamb was to be broken; it had to be roasted whole. Nearly 1500 years before the crucifixion of Jesus God knew that not a bone of his body would be broken (Exodus 12:9 & 46b; John 19:31-34).

The Manna – A Type of Jesus The Bread Of Life.

The people murmured against Moses in the wilderness and complained bitterly that there was nothing to eat (Exodus ch.16). The Lord promised bread from heaven and this was to be an excellent type of Jesus the Bread of Heaven (John 6:25-56).

The miracle of the manna was provided every day except for the Sabbath day (Exodus 16:21-23) but enough was gathered on the sixth day to last the people over the Sabbath. This was a further miracle, for on other days if too much was gathered it did not keep (16:20). Jesus our Saviour, our Living Bread, was provided for us through the miracle of his virgin birth (Matthew 1:20b).

They did not know what the manna was (Exodus 16:15), In the original Hebrew word for manna, *mahu*, means either, 'What is this?' or, *manan*, 'This is a gift!' – The ingredients of the manna were unknown and this is a type of God's secret design coming to fruition in the combination of the two natures of Christ.

One of his names was called '*Wonderful*'; (Isaiah 9:6) and this is equivalent to 'secret' in the Hebrew language. This word is also used in Judges where his name is translated as '*beyond understanding*' (Judges 13:18).

The manna came from heaven (Exodus 16:4). It was a supernatural provision for each day coming down with the dew in the mornings. Jesus declared he had come down from heaven, indeed he told the Jews seven times in John chapter 6 that he came from heaven so that we could have eternal life (John 6:33, 38, 46, 50, 51, 58, 61). It is fascinating also that Paul gives us seven steps in our Lord's descent from heaven to earth and then to his death in Philippians –

> '*Who being in very nature God, did not consider equality with God something to be grasped,(1) but made himself nothing,(2) taking the very nature of a servant, (3) being made in human likeness. And (4) being found in appearance as a man, (5) he humbled himself and (6) became obedient to death (7) even death on a cross!*' (Philippians 2:6-8).

The manna resembled flakes of frost (Exodus 16:14). Transparent and semi-crystal, a flake of frost reminds us of Jesus who is like the pure river of the water of life, clear as crystal (Revelation 22:1), He is holy (Mark 1:24; Luke 1:35; Acts 3:14), and we must guard our steps when we go into his presence, always remembering that we are dust. We should not take him for granted even though he loves us so much, but we should stand in awe of him (Ecclesiastes 5:1-7). Meditation on his glory, his throne, his power, and his kingship will maintain our respect toward him.

The manna tasted like wafers made with honey (Exodus 16:31). In Jewish tradition it is said that the manna tasted differently to each person, for example in the Jewish apocryphal book of Wisdom we find –

> *By contrast, thy own people were given angel's food, and thou didst send them from heaven, without labour of their own, bread ready to eat, rich in delight of every kind and suited to every taste* (Wisdom 16:20).

As Jesus, since his resurrection, is now once again omni-present he is able to know us and be with us individually. We are under his tender care and we should not hesitate to bring to him our every concern for he cares for us (1Peter 5:7). William Barclay brings that care into focus when he says, 'God loves each one of us as if there was only one of us to love.'[17]

The manna tasted like olive oil (Numbers 11:8b), A type of the Holy Spirit, this oil reminds us that Jesus was born through the agency of the Holy Spirit and empowered by him (John 1:32 & 3:34). As we pray and meditate; as we worship, the Holy Spirit enlarges our understanding of Jesus. As we take in the wonder of who he is in his perfection and nobility of character he transforms us from glory to glory (2 Corinthians 3:17-18).

It melted when the sun grew hot (Exodus 16:21), Gathering the manna in the early morning was essential for it melted away as the day progressed. We in turn should seek the Lord when we are young, not leaving our surrender to him until we are old and worn

---

[17] Barclay, William; *The Daily Study Bible*; 'The Gospel of Luke'; The St. Andrew Press; Edinburgh. Pg. 114

out. On a daily basis also it is best to seek the Lord in the early morning for our spiritual food for the day (Psalm 5:3; 34:1).

The Israelites were completely dependent on God for their daily supply of manna and we too need to have an attitude of complete surrender to God for our daily needs. He will give us grace each time we need it (Hebrews 4:14-16).

As Christians, we in turn must share what we receive from the Lord. We learn dependence on God through suffering and trial then we become broken bread by sharing our lives and God's grace with others in need.

The manna fell in abundance and there was enough for everyone (Exodus 16:17). Mathematicians have worked out that over the forty years of the wilderness wanderings of the children of Israel, God must have provided literally millions of litres of manna. Such an abundance of provision indicates that Jesus who is the Living Bread is sufficient for every man, woman and child who has ever lived, or will live, on this planet of ours. It is not God's will that any should be left out of the plan of salvation (2 Peter 3:9).

The manna was loathed while they were at Hormah (Numbers 21:5b). They said, *'We detest this miserable food.'* Jesus too was despised and rejected by men and he was crucified because of their implacable hatred (Isaiah 53:3).

It was kept in a pot for a memorial (Exodus 16:32-34). An omer (4.25 litres) of manna was collected on the Lord's command and put into a jar to be preserved for future generations. Jesus promises hidden manna to the overcomer (Revelation 2:17) and he himself is hidden in the heavenlies, seated on the throne at his Father's right hand, until the moment of his return in glory with his holy angels (Revelation 1:7).

So the manna was a type of Christ but by itself it cannot fully describe all that he is. Jesus is indeed the Bread of Life, sufficient for all our needs. Jesus would never have said the things about himself (revealed in John chapter six) if he had not known that he was the eternal Son of God.

He said *'I am the resurrection and the life'* (John 11:25), the manna gave only physical life but Jesus gives life eternal, the very life of God, to all who believe in him (6:51).

When we take the bread and the cup at communion we do two things: *first,* we receive by faith the forgiveness of our sins; and *second,* by faith we receive grace to maintain our Christian life. This grace is freely given to us by God for all time (1Corinthians 11:23-32).

The Pillar of Cloud and Of Fire – A Symbol of Jesus.

During the desert evenings, when in the camp of the Israelites all activity ceased, the pillar of cloud and fire settled down over the tabernacle where the Ark of the Covenant lay. In the early morning, if God decreed it was time to move on, the pillar of cloud would lift and move ahead of the people (Numbers 9:15-23). Moses established a ritual that he kept night and morning.

> *The cloud of the Lord was over them by day when they set out from the camp. Whenever the ark set out, Moses said, 'Rise up, O Lord! May your enemies be scattered; may your foes flee before you.' Whenever it came to rest, he said, 'Return O Lord, to the countless thousands of Israel'* (Numbers 10:34-36).

The pillar was a guide for them from the first, a pillar of fire by night became a pillar of cloud by day. The journey which should have taken only two weeks turned into 40 years of testing and trial. The cloud went before them and led them on each day, it was a defence (Exodus 14:19-20) and a shelter (Numbers 10:33-34) and it stayed with them until the end of the journey (Exodus 13:22; Isaiah 58:11; 1 Peter 5:7).

Jesus is our guide, *'His sheep follow him because they know his voice'* (John 10:3b). We are also told that he will be our guard against anxiety (Philippians 4:4-7) and also our victorious Saviour

(Ephesians 4:8). He will shelter us underneath his wings and we will be able to rest in his shadow –

> *He who dwells in the shelter of the Most High will rest in the shadow of the Almighty. I will say of the Lord, 'He is my refuge and my fortress, my God, in whom I trust'* (Psalm 91:1-2).

The Red Sea – Water Baptism.

The Red Sea is a symbol of our baptism in water. In 1Corinthians 10:1-2 we read the confirmation of this type as Paul refers to the Israelites being baptised into Moses in the cloud and in the sea (Exodus ch.14). There are many other similarities between the pilgrimage of Israel and Christian life. Those I have collected over the years are listed briefly here:

- The Egyptian Bondage (Exodus 1:11-14) – A type of the bondage of sin.
- Moses as a Deliverer (Exodus 6:1-8) – A type of Christ.
- The Exodus (Exodus 13:3-10) – A type of the abandonment of the sinful life.
- The Passover Lamb (Exodus 12:1-30) – A type of Christ, the Lamb of God
- Pharaoh's Pursuit of Israel (Exodus 14:5-14) – A type of the evil forces pursuing believers.
- The Opening of the Red Sea (Exodus 14:21) - A type of hindrances removed.
- The Pillar of Cloud and Fire (Exodus 14:19-20) – A type of the Jesus' presence with believers and his guiding hand on their lives,
- The Song of Moses (Exodus 15:1-18) – A type of our Songs of spiritual victory (Colossians 3:16-17).

- The Mixed Multitude (Exodus 12:38) – A type of the worldly element in the church.
- Marah and Elim (Exodus 15:22-27) – A type of the bitter and sweet experiences of the religious life.
- The Flesh Pots (Exodus 16:3) – A type of the sensual pleasures of the old life.
- The Manna (Exodus 16:4) – A type of Christ, the Bread of Life.
- The Water from the Rock (Exodus 17:5-7) – A type of Christ the Living Water.
- The Upholding of Moses' Hands (Exodus 17:10-13) – A type of the need for co-operation with leaders.

The Healing Tree – A Type of The Cross

Wilderness experiences that we go through in our Christian life are permitted to test how strong is our relationship with God, how much we trust him and rely on him; how unshakable is our faith in his Word (Deuteronomy 8:2). The tree, which Moses cast into the bitter water (Exodus 15:22-27) was a type of the cross of Christ that changes our lives and turns that which is bitter and twisted into something sweet, orderly, and disciplined (Acts 5:30-32; Galatians 5;22-26). We cannot change the past nor eradicate our mistakes, but Christ can recycle the past and use it somehow for the furtherance of his will for our lives; he can take the sting from the bitterest memories and comfort us by using what we have learned from them for his purposes (Psalm 66:8-10; 1Peter 5:10-11).

The Smitten Rock – The Saviour.

This rock at Horeb is a type of our Saviour, and the water that gushed out after Moses struck it is a type of the water of life that flows from Christ to satisfy the thirsty soul (Exodus 17:6). The type here is that Christ was to be struck, but only once! He died once for all.

In Jeremiah God calls himself a spring of living water (Jeremiah 2:13-14; 17:13). In Isaiah God has promised that it is with joy that we will draw water from the wells of salvation (Isaiah 12:3). Jesus has promised that if we drink of him we will never thirst again (John 4:13-14). Then finally we will live, along with all the saints, by the waters of the river of life where the tree of life grows in the Kingdom of God (Revelation 22:1-5). So water is a very important symbol of the everlasting life that we have been promised.

The second rock at Kadesh (Numbers 20:6-13) was struck twice by Moses in anger. God had told him to speak only to the rock but he was so angry with the people that he struck the rock instead. Moses and Aaron both paid a bitter price for this. They were forbidden by God to enter the Promised Land, for a leader is judged more strictly than those who are not in leadership (James 3:1), The Saviour was to be smitten only once, he was to die only once, so it was very important for Moses merely to *speak* to this second rock (1 Peter 3:18).

Aaron's Rod That Budded – Christ's Resurrection.

The story behind this miraculous event (Numbers 17:8) was the rebellion of certain Levites. They were not content with the tasks for which God had designed them but were determined to take on the ministry of priests in place of Aaron and his sons (Numbers ch.16). They opposed Moses (16:3), they grumbled about their situation (vs. 10, 11), and they were defiant against the God-given authority placed in Moses and Aaron (vs.12-14). God moved against these men because of these sins and they were destroyed. The very next day there was more rebellion in the camp, this time from the whole assembly. God dealt with this rebellion also and then he decided to show the people once and for all who were his chosen leaders. Each tribal leader had to produce his staff and write his name on it and Aaron had to add his staff also. All the staffs were then taken into the Tent of the Testimony and placed before the Lord. Miraculously Aaron's Rod not only sprouted, but it budded, blossomed, and produced almonds!

This was kept thereafter in the Ark of the Covenant, along with the Ten Commandments and the portion of manna, as a sign to the rebellious. We are warned in 1 Corinthians 10:1-13 and in Hebrews 3:12-19 that we should not be guilty of the sins of the ancient Israelites, of their grumbling and rebellion against God. Moses did not take on himself the position of leadership of God's people, nor did Aaron take on himself the honour of fulfilling the position of high priest, they were both of them God's appointments.

Aaron's rod that budded is a symbol of Christ's resurrection. Jesus has risen and lives forever, now chosen by God to be our High Priest (Hebrews 5:1-6). In heaven he continues to intercede for us before the Father (Hebrews 7:24-25).

The Brazen Serpent – Christ's Death on the Cross

Once more impatience, grumbling and open rebellion bring the judgment of God on the Israelites. But as the poisonous snakes begin to kill the people God instructs Moses to make a way of escape for them (Numbers 21:6-9). Moses sets up the brazen snake on the pole and all the people have only to look on the snake to be cured (Numbers 21:9). This brazen serpent is a symbol of Christ who was to come and be offered up on a cross for our salvation. All we have to do is look to him and be saved. Jesus confirmed this –

> *Just as Moses lifted up the snake in the desert, so the Son of Man must be lifted up, that everyone who believes in him may have eternal life* (John 3:14,15).

The Six Cities of Refuge – Christ Our Refuge and Strength

In different ways these cities bring to light aspects of Christ. In Bible days the law was, '*an eye for an eye and a tooth for a tooth.*' If a man committed manslaughter he was in danger from the family of the man he had accidently killed (Joshua 20:1-6). The cities of refuge then were for his protection and you can imagine the scene. First, the horror of the accident, then the full realisation of the death of the victim and what that could mean. Knowing this the perpetrator would run as swiftly as he could to the nearest city of refuge to preserve his life from the victim's family who would be swift in seeking revenge. There was little mercy in those days!

Here are the cities and their various meanings which point to aspects of Christ our Saviour–

Kedesh: the name of this city in Galilee means 'holy place' and it comes from a root word meaning 'sanctify', and Jesus our Saviour was born holy and uncorrupted by sin as Gabriel explained to Mary –.

> *'The Holy Spirit will come upon you and the power of the Most High will overshadow you. So the holy one to be born will be called the Son of God'* (Luke 1:35; cp Psalm 16:9-10).

Shechem: this city was in Mt Ephraim and the word means 'back' or 'shoulder' from the root word 'strength' or 'to burden'. Jesus is strong and will protect and guide us through every difficulty (Isaiah 9:6-7).

> *I will place on his shoulder the key to the house of David; what he opens no one can shut, and what he shuts no one can open* (Isaiah 22:22).

Here the primary reference is to Eliakim son of Hilkiah (Isaiah 22:20), but we know that Jesus will eventually grasp the key to the house of David and he will be the one who rules. No one will be able to shut a door that he opens or open a door that he closes.

Kirjath Arba (that is Hebron): the name of this city, situated in Judah, means 'confederation' or 'communion'. This comes from an origin suggesting 'association or 'fellowship.' We are invited to have fellowship with the Lord on a daily basis. How privileged we are, as John points out in his first letter –

> *We proclaim to you what we have seen and heard, so that you also may have fellowship with us. And our fellowship is with the Father and with his Son, Jesus Christ* (1 John 1:3).

Bezer; located in the wilderness, this city's name means 'a fortification' or 'a stronghold'. It comes from a word meaning 'to hew as from a quarry.' Surely the Lord is our refuge and strength, and he is ready to help us when we are in trouble and cry out to him in our distress.

> *The Lord is my rock, my fortress and my deliverer; my God is my rock, in whom I take refuge* (Psalm 18:2a; cp. Zechariah 9:12 & Nahum 1:7).

Ramoth: in Gilead, means 'height' or 'eminence'. It comes from a word meaning 'to be lofty' or 'exultation'. Our Lord is indeed exulted to the highest place and reigns in glory at his Father's right hand.

> *Great is the Lord in Zion; he is exalted over all the nations* (Psalm 99:2).

Golan: this city, built in Bashan, has a name some scholars say means 'happy' or 'joy'. Others that it means 'circle' or 'revolution'. No matter, this word also can lead us to Christ. He is willing to surround our lives with his love and keep us safe from harm and danger. He also gives us joy in the Holy Spirit.

> *Whoever gives heed to instruction prospers, and blessed is he who trusts in the Lord* (Proverbs 16:20). *The joy of the Lord is your strength* (Nehemiah 8:10b). *The angel of the Lord encamps around those who fear him, and he delivers them* (Psalm 34:7).

Those cities numbered six in all and this number in the Bible stands for 'man.' Christ is indeed our refuge and strength in times of trouble. We can run to him and seek refuge from trouble or danger (Psalm 46:1; Romans 8:31-39).

The Twelve Stones –

The first stones symbolise the cross, the second set, our new life in Christ.

Joshua promised the Israelites that as the priests went ahead carrying the ark of the Lord into the river Jordan that its waters flowing downstream would be cut off and stand in a heap (Joshua 3:13). And so it happened. The priests continued to stand in the midst of the stream while the whole tribe passed over. The picked men, one from each tribe, gathered twelve stones from the bank of the stream and placed them in the river where the priests had stood so that the people could go over dry shod (4:9). Those twelve stones taken from the river bank typify the cross of Christ and remind us that we were baptised into his death (Romans 6:3-14).

Then Joshua commanded that another twelve stones were to be gathered from the river bed where the priests stood and put down where the Israelites were to camp that night. When Joshua set them up in Gilgal (Joshua 4:20), over the river into the promised land, they spoke of our new resurrection life in Christ (Ephesians 2:4-10).

Chapter Five:

Cameos Of Christ

God's Wonderful Plan

Some people find it incomprehensible that God should require the sacrifice of animals and then in time the death of his Son to free us from sin. Some even dare to say God was cruel to expect his Son to die for us. However they should realise that God himself was in Christ, suffering along with him for our salvation. With our limited understanding we cannot fathom the depth of the pain suffered by the Godhead to rescue his people from death. God planned it all, knowing there was no other way to compass our redemption.

There is a reasonable explanation of the need for Jesus' death on the cross.

- ♦ **First and foremost God loves us** and wants to have fellowship with us (Revelation 3:20), but because he is a Holy God and cannot look upon sin, he cannot have friendship with us unless we are perfect as he is perfect (Matthew 5:48).

- ♦ **Not one of us is perfect**, and we cannot become perfect except through the blood of Jesus; for we have all sinned and come short of the glory of God (Romans 3:23).

- ♦ **We can never be good enough by our own efforts** no matter how hard we try, so God has provided a way for us to be good enough through Jesus our Saviour (John 3:16). He is the connection between us and God, the bridge over which we can cross to the Kingdom of God.

- ♦ **Once we have accepted Jesus** and his sacrifice for us God sees us as forgiven and clothed in God's righteousness. Now we can have fellowship and friendship with God and nothing can separate us from his love (Romans 8: 35-39).

The tabernacle in the wilderness abounds with types and shadows of the sacrifice of Christ who was to come, and these prove once again that God knew and planned everything in minute detail ahead of time.

Types from the Tabernacle

When God gave the pattern of the tabernacle to Moses we note that he began with the description of the ark of the covenant with its mercy seat, that part of the tabernacle within the Holy of Holies closest to himself and his glory (Exodus 25:8-22). As fallen human beings in need of a Saviour, we must begin at the other end of the tabernacle furnishings, with the brazen altar of sacrifice (Exodus 27:1-8). Studying the various furniture of the Tabernacle we can see from New Testament references that they were each in some way representative of Jesus who was to come.

For instance, beginning with chapter one of John's gospel we can see his whole book is set out in line with the Tabernacle. Starting with the Lamb of God in chapter one and moving forward through the chapters Jesus identifies himself as living water, the light of the world, the bread of life, and so on. We will see as we continue that these aspects of Jesus correspond to parts of the tabernacle furnishings. This is either a deliberate act on John's part or else a divine intervention by the Holy Spirit. However planned, it is certainly an extraordinary and wonderful confirmation of how the Bible fits together despite the thousands of years separating the different authors.

The following table will give a quick review of the correlation between the parts of the tabernacle and the characteristics of Jesus in John's gospel.

The Altar of Sacrifice	Jesus as the Lamb of God (John 1:29-36).
The Laver	Jesus the Water of life (3:5; 7:37-49).
The Table of Shewbread	Jesus the Bread of life (6: 35).
The Seven Branched Candlestick	Jesus the Light of the World (8:12; 9:4-5).
The Altar of Incense	Jesus' Teaching and Prayers (chs. 14 &17).
The Mercy Seat	Jesus on the Cross (19:28-37).
The Shekinah Glory	Jesus gives the Holy Spirit (20:21-23).

The Brazen Altar of Sacrifice

The commands given to Moses concerning the sacrifices were specifically to allow the people, many of whom could not read or write, a colourful, visual image of what God required from them if they wanted a relationship with their Holy, All-wise, All-knowing, Ever-present and Almighty God.

In Exodus the brazen altar of sacrifice indicates that the only way for sinful man to approach a holy God is through sacrifice (Exodus 27:1-8; 38:1-7).

Twice in chapter one of John's gospel, John the Baptist speaks of the Lamb of God and this refers in type to the brazen altar. When John saw Jesus coming toward him he said, *'Look, the Lamb of God, who takes away the sin of the world'* (John 1:29-36).

The Laver

The brass laver contained the sacred water for the cleansing of those who ministered and it speaks to us of the need for spiritual renewal. The washing of the hands of the priests symbolises our

Christian conduct, and the washing of the feet of the priests symbolises our Christian walk (Exodus 30:17-21; 38:8).

In chapter three of his gospel, John speaks of the new birth and indicates we must be born of water and the Spirit.

> *Jesus answered, 'I tell you the truth, no one can enter the kingdom of God unless he is born of water and the Spirit'* (John 3:5)

The water of the brass laver in the Old Testament indicates our need for the water of God, symbolised by the Spirit of God –

> *On the last and greatest day of the Feast, Jesus stood and said in a loud voice, 'If anyone is thirsty, let him come to me and drink. Whoever believes in me, as the Scripture has said, streams of living water will flow from within him.' By this he meant the Spirit, whom those who believed in him were later to receive* (John 7:37-39a).

The Table of Shewbread

The table of shewbread with the bread of God's presence represents Jesus who was to come as the bread of life. He came that we might have eternal, spiritual life. The table was placed within the Holy Place on the right hand (north) and included plates, dishes, and bowls for the bread and pitchers for the drink offering (Exodus 25:23-30; 37:10-16).

In type the table of shewbread is referred to in John chapters four and six where we read of living water and living bread.

> *Jesus answered, 'Everyone who drinks this water will be thirsty again, but whoever drinks the water I give him will never thirst. Indeed, the water I give him will become in him a spring of water welling up to eternal life'* (John 4:13-14).

> *Then Jesus declared, 'I am the bread of life, he who comes to me will never go hungry, and he who believes in me will never be thirsty'* (John 6:35).

The Seven-Branched Candle Stick

The seven-branched candlestick with its elaborate and beautiful patterns is described next. This is another symbol of Jesus and speaks to us of spiritual revelation from the Lord (Exodus 25:31-40; 37:17-24).

In John's gospel, chapters eight and nine, Jesus refers to himself as the Light of the World.

> *When Jesus spoke again to the people, he said, 'I am the light of the world. Whoever follows me will never walk in darkness, but will have the light of life'* (John 8:12).

> *As long as it is day, we must do the work of him who sent me. Night is coming, when no one can work. While I am in the world, I am the light of the world* (9:4-5).

The Altar of Incense

There is some ambiguity in Exodus chapter 25 as to the altar of incense. It seems that the table of shewbread and the altar of incense are mentioned here together, because along with the bowls and plates for the table we read of the incense to be offered. We read later in Exodus chapter 30 that the golden altar of incense was a separate altar and it was to be placed before the curtain which separated the Holy of Holies from the Holy Place and hid the mercy seat ((Exodus 30:1-10; 37:25-28).. When the incense was burned on this altar and the smoke of the incense rose in the air it symbolised the prayers and supplications of the people of God (Revelation 8:3-4).

The name for 'altar' meant 'place of slaughter', and so it is interesting that the 'altar' of incense had the same designation as the 'altar' of sacrifice. This indicates that our prayers are only acceptable through the sacrifice of Calvary. The blood from the altar of sacrifice had also to be taken and placed on the horns of the altar of incense. The horns speak of power and strength and indicate in type that the priestly power of our Saviour comes from his death on Calvary.

The altar of incense is indicated in John's gospel by the teaching of Jesus on prayer (John ch.14) and by his wonderful prayer for his disciples and for all future believers (ch. 17).

> (Jesus said), *'And I will do whatever you ask in my name, so that the Son may bring glory to the Father. You may ask me for anything in my name, and I will do it'* (John 14:13-14)
>
> *My prayer is not for them alone. I pray also for those who will believe in me through their message, that all of them may be one, Father, just as you are in me and I am in you. May they also be in us so that the world may believe that you have sent me* (17:20-21).

The Incense

The study of the four ingredients of the incense burned on the altar of incense show some remarkable types of the character of the Christ who was to come.

Stacte, or gum resin, is a powder taken from the centre of hardened drops of myrrh, it is rare and costly. Myrrh is obtained by the crushing and distilling of the whole bush, flowers, leaves, and branches. Christ himself is indeed rare, he is the One and Only Son of God (John 1:14). The crushing and distilling and the fact that every part of the myrrh is used indicates the suffering through which Christ was to pass during his trial and crucifixion. He was crushed and wounded for us (Isaiah 53:5).

Onycha is made from mollusc shells found in the Red Sea. They emit a penetrating odour when burnt. The shells would have been crushed to make them suitable for mixing with the other ingredients of the incense. The pounding of the shells can remind us again of the incredible sufferings of the Saviour, who was bruised and torn and nailed to a cross for us (John 19).

Galbanum is a rubbery resin that is harvested from the roots of a flowering plant that thrives in Syria and Persia (now Iran). As this root was hidden in the earth we see a type of Christ in whom are hidden all the treasures of wisdom and knowledge (Colossians 2:2-3).

Frankincense is a resin that comes from the bark of Boswellia Carteri, a herb, which grows in Southern Arabia. The word *tahore* (purity), is used when referring to the 'pure frankincense' used. This indicates the purity of the character of Christ. He was the 'holy one' to be born of the virgin Mary (Luke 1:35) and he remained spotless all the days of his earthly journey. Frankincense also speaks of death as it was used to embalm a body after death, so it speaks of the death that Christ was to suffer for us (Psalm 22:14-18).

The ingredients could have been part of the riches that were given to the Israelites by the Egyptians before their final exodus. If this is the case then it would explain their possession of the four ingredients and their ability to prepare this costly incense for the tabernacle.

> *Then the Lord said to Moses, 'Take fragrant spices – gum resin, onycha and galbanum – and pure frankincense, all in equal amounts, and make a fragrant blend of incense, the work of a perfumer. It is to be salted and pure and sacred* (Exodus 30:34-35).

Salted and pure and sacred the incense was to be prepared in portions that were of equal weight. This speaks to us of the balanced perfection of Christ. He was holy, finely balanced emotionally, and mature in his character, the living Word of God incarnate. His whole life was governed and made fragrant by his obedience to his heavenly Father.

The beautiful aroma of the incense was produced by the pounding it received in pestle and mortar (Exodus 30:36) and this points to the suffering of Christ and his faithful completion of his Father's will (Matthew 25:21; John 17:4).

The incense was also burnt with fire (Leviticus 16:13) and this surely speaks of the cross and the trial through which Jesus walked, setting his face like a flint (Isaiah 50:7) to go through his agony to ultimate victory. As the incense was burnt and the fragrance reached up to envelop the worshippers it reminds us of the intercessions of Christ. As our great High Priest he stands at the right hand of the Father making intercession for us who believe.

The incense was unique for no one was permitted to make it for personal use. If they did they faced punishment. We in turn are unable to manufacture our own righteousness, we cannot do anything for ourselves to gain cleansing, it must all come to us freely from the Father and from Jesus, the Son, our Saviour and Lord (Isaiah 55:1-3). We cannot earn our own salvation: if we try, then our efforts are as filthy rags in the sight of God (64:6).

Incense, in the Bible, is typical of prayer:

> *O Lord, I call to you; come quickly to me. Hear my voice when I call to you. May my prayer be set before you like incense* (Psalm 141:1-2).

> *The four living creatures and the twenty four elders fell down before the Lamb. Each one had a harp and they were holding golden bowls full of incense, which are the prayers of the saints* (Revelation 5:8).

> *Another angel, who had a golden censer, came and stood at the altar. He was given much incense to offer, with the prayers of all the saints, on the golden altar before the throne* (8:3).

The beautiful aroma arising from the golden altar of incense is a type not only of our prayers but also of Jesus, our great High Priest, who makes intercession before the Father on our behalf (Hebrews 7:23-25).

Our worship, praise and service to God are also likened to incense:

> *I am amply supplied, now that I have received from Epaphroditus the gifts you sent. They are a fragrant offering,*

an acceptable sacrifice, pleasing to God (Philippians 4:18b-19*)*.

And do not forget to do good and to share with others, for with such sacrifices God is pleased (Hebrews 13:16).

You also, like living stones, are being built into a spiritual house to be a holy priesthood, offering spiritual sacrifices acceptable to God through Jesus Christ (1 Peter 2:5).

The incense had to be mixed with the fire from the altar of sacrifice. As Nadab and Abihu discovered to their destruction no other fire was acceptable (Leviticus 10:1-10). We must be careful in view of this that we base our life and service for God on the sacrifice of Christ and his precious blood. No other foundation will do; we dare not base our prayers on our own efforts.

When the morning and evening sacrifices were placed on the brazen altar, fresh incense was placed in the censer upon the golden altar of incense (Exodus 30:7-8). Because of this timing a strange and wonderful scenario must have arisen at the time our Saviour died on the cross. He was placed on the cross at nine in the morning (the third hour) and remained there for six hours. His death took place at three in the afternoon (the ninth hour) at the time of evening prayer (Acts 3:1). The priest rostered for duty that day must have been offering incense at the very moment Jesus committed his spirit to his Father, therefore the curtain covering the Holy of Holies must have been split in two right before the eyes of the officiating priest (Luke 23:44-46; Matthew 27:45-51).

The hour of the Lord's death was foretold in type by the daily offering of the incense and by the timing of the evening offering. The day was foretold in the Passover, and the year of his death in Daniel's prophecy as we saw in chapter three of this book (Daniel 9:25-26).

The Mercy Seat

The golden ark must have been very beautiful with its two cherubim with their wings spread over the mercy seat. It was here the high priest sprinkled the blood of the atonement so long ago. This application of blood to the mercy seat once each year was a looking forward to the sacrifice Jesus would finally accomplish for us on the cross (Exodus 25:9-22; 37:1-9).

The mercy seat is indicated in John chapter 20 when Jesus was about to return to heaven after his resurrection. He told Mary Magdalene not to hold onto him as he had to return to his Father and complete his mission by sprinkling his own blood on the mercy seat of God's heavenly tabernacle.

> *Jesus said, 'Do not hold onto me, for I have not yet ascended to the Father. Go instead to my brothers and tell them, 'I am returning to my Father and your Father, to my God and your God'* (John 20:17)

In the evening of that same day the Shekinah glory, the Holy Spirit, which used to hover over the mercy seat between the cherubim, was breathed on the disciples. Jesus indicated that in giving them the Holy Spirit he was ensuring their entrance into a new relationship with God which would change their lives.

> *Again Jesus said, 'Peace be with you! As the Father has sent me, I am sending you.' And he breathed on them and said, 'Receive the Holy Spirit. If you forgive anyone his sins, they are forgiven; if you do not forgive them, they are not forgiven'* (John 20:21-23).

Later, while in prayer in the upper room in Jerusalem, the disciples were finally to receive the Baptism of the Holy Spirit and power (Acts 2:4).

The Five Sacrifices

Just as God began to describe the furniture of the Tabernacle, from the Holy of Holies working out to the altar of sacrifice, so with the offerings, God begins with the one nearest to his heart.

We therefore must begin with the fifth and last of the offerings written down for us, the trespass offering, and progress upward to the first offering, an individual expression of devotion, thanksgiving and worship to God. **Even though the old sacrifices have been repealed and are no longer necessary**, still, if taken in reverse order, the sacrifices show us in type the upward progress of our Christian life.

Before we begin however, we should note that in these sacrifices there was to be no sacrifice for wilful, deliberate sin committed by anyone (Numbers 15:30-31), only for sins committed in ignorance (Leviticus ch.4)

It is not clear however, what wilful deliberate sin entails. Barnes comments:

> The heavy punishments which had already overtaken the people might naturally give rise to apprehensions for the future, especially in view of the fact that on the approaching entrance into Canaan the complete observance of the Law in all its details would become imperative on them. To meet such apprehensions a distinction is emphatically drawn between sins of ignorance (Lev 4:13 ff.), and those of presumption (Num 15:30-31). The passage deals separately with imperfections of obedience which would be regarded as attaching to the whole nation (Num 15:22-26), and those of individuals (Num 15:27-30).[18]

So we see that these sins of ignorance, or presumption were linked to disobedience of the Law on the part of individuals or on the part of the whole nation of Israel. However, in the New Testament also we are solemnly reminded that if we deliberately keep on sinning after we have come to the knowledge of the truth, no sacrifice for sins is left (Hebrews 10:26).

The Trespass Offering

This was **the trespass (guilt) offering** and it had two sections, one toward God and the other toward our fellowman. Jesus died that

---

[18] Barnes, Albert. *Commentary on the Old Testament; in loc.*

we might regain fellowship with a Holy God and restore fellowship with our brothers and sisters in Christ. We begin with feelings of guilt, then we repent and receive forgiveness for our sins, going on to restore and make things right with God and our neighbour (Leviticus 7:1-10).

The Sin Offering

The sin offering was for everyone, high or low born, all had to repent of their sin and accept the sacrifice of atonement. Jesus Christ is our effectual sin offering, he gave his life voluntarily that we might be set free from sin and live unto God. With this offering we begin to realise that it is not only our visible, outward sin but the root of sin in our life which needs to be dealt with (Leviticus 6:25-30).

The Peace Offering

The peace (fellowship) offering was food for the priest and the worshipper alike, and this sacrifice represents Christ who is not only our Saviour but the source of our spiritual food. As we read and meditate on the Word of God each day we mature in our spiritual life and we gain a wonderful peace that passes understanding. The Lord reveals himself to us and we are reconciled to him (Leviticus 7:11-21).

The Meal Offering

The meal (grain) offering was a voluntary thanksgiving offering. Sometimes cooked into bread wafers, this offering was made from a man's work of cultivation. In a sense he was acknowledging God's goodness and help in his life. In this state we find rest and joy and complete acceptance with God in the glorious perfections of Christ. We know now we can do nothing ourselves, we must totally depend on him (Leviticus 6:14-28).

The Whole Burnt Offering

The whole burnt offering was an individual expression of devotion, thanksgiving, and of worship to God. It could consist of a bull, sheep, goat, pigeon or turtledove. No matter how poor the individual, they could offer what they had. This offering speaks to us of the total commitment of Jesus who gave himself for us. We come into deeper and deeper fellowship with God through the fullness of the perfect offering, which is Christ our Saviour (Leviticus 6:8-13).

There are many more symbols and types that scholars have enjoyed discovering in the tabernacle as a whole and in the various sacrifices and offerings. Those who are interested can get these books and enjoy studying the details.

Suggested reading:

Chant, Barry *Typology,* Vision Publishing; Ramona CA

Slemming, C.W. *Thus Shalt Thou Serve* and *These Are The Garments,* Christian Literature Crusade, Fort Washington, Pennsylvania 1974.

Lockyer, Herbert; *All the Messianic Prophecies of the Bible;* Zondervan Publishing; Grand Rapids Mi.; 1973.

Baxter, Sidlow J. Explore the Book; Volume One; Marshall, Morgan and Scott, Ltd. 1951; Pg. 53.

Chapter Six:

Pictures Of Christ

Prophetic Pictures

The following studies show prophetic pictures of Christ found in Old Testament characters. Not all aspects of their lives depict parts of Christ's life and character therefore we must be careful to differentiate between what is confirmed by the New Testament and what is not proved.

As in chapter five some of these types will be directly related and acknowledged in the New Testament, others will be of interest only and show how the whole Bible charmingly indicates aspects of Christ throughout its pages.

Adam — Adam Represents The Old Creation, Christ The New Creation.

In Adam we see the head, the beginning of God's original creation, which fell into sin (Genesis ch. 3), and in Christ we see the head, the beginning of God's new creation who, because of his sinless life and death on the cross, restored us to God's grace and forgiveness (1 Corinthians 15:22,45; Romans 5:17-19).

Abel — A Type of The Innocent Christ

In Abel an innocent man is murdered by his brother (Genesis 4:1-16) as Jesus was murdered by his Jewish brethren. Abel heads the list of men of faith in Hebrews chapter 11, By faith he offered a better sacrifice than Cain did, for it was his heart attitude that pleased God. By faith he was commended as a righteous man, but the blood of Jesus Christ our mediator speaks a better word to us (Hebrews 12:24).

Melchizedek – A Type of Christ As Both King and High Priest

Melchizedek was king of Salem and he brought out bread and wine for Abraham, blessing him in his role as priest. In turn Abraham gave him a tenth of everything he had won in battle (Genesis 14:17-20). As both priest and king, Melchizedek is a type of Jesus, who is both King of kings and our great High Priest who intercedes for us before the Father.

Who was Melchizedek? His name means, 'king of righteousness'; and king of Salem means, 'king of peace'. These names reveal him as a representative of Jesus, King of kings, who is our righteousness and our peace (Hebrews 7:1-2, 24-25). The reference in Hebrews to Melchizedek having neither father nor mother, nor genealogy is interesting. Some Jewish scholars believe it is possible he could have been Shem, one of Noah's sons, who would still have been alive at this time. Shem was one hundred years of age when he became a father and lived after this a further 500 years. His life spanned 600 years in all, so he would still have been living in the time of Abraham (Genesis 11:10-11). However, as it cannot be proved that Melchizedek was Shem this must remain an interesting legend only.

Abraham – A Type of The Fatherhood of God

John Newton was one of England's prominent Christian leaders and the writer of that famous hymn *'Amazing Grace.'* In letters written to friends he taught three distinct phases of the Christian life. They were desire, conflict and contemplation:

Desire; 'The believer in this stage resembles a child, genuine in his zeal for Christ but susceptible to falling away when trouble comes or he fails and sins.

Conflict; 'In this stage the believer enters manhood, though still young and untried. His trials are sharper and more difficult, and through spiritual warfare this Christian comes to know the deceitfulness of his own heart – and consequently, praises the greater mercy of Christ.

Contemplation: 'Having experienced the grace of God through trials and failures, the believer at this stage enters what Newton calls fatherhood. Here the Christian no longer trusts his own heart, but dwells more fully on the redeeming love and glory of God.'[19]

In contemplating the life of Abraham we can see him living through these three stages as a sincere Christian believer does today.

Abram, as he was before God gave him the new name, Abraham, lived a life of faith and it was counted to him for righteousness, we too must live a life of faith, believing in the finished work of Christ.

In every faith walk there is first a testing. God needs to examine our lives to see if we are ready for his blessing and the task he has for us. Will we give him all the glory? Trials are seasonal, and how we react to the testing will determine whether or not the blessing comes.

Stage one (desire): Abram reached out to God and was obedient to his call (Genesis 12:1-5).

He was promised blessing, then immediately after the promise came the testing time. A famine came on the land (12:10). Abram could go back home, he could believe God for provision, or he could go to Egypt.

His reaction was a self-centered one, 'What is best for me and mine?' He went down to Egypt and in doing so selfishly risked Sarai's life (12:10-20). He failed the test, but God did not cast him off!

---

[19] Newton, John. *A Believer's Progress;* Christian History Magazine, Issue 81; Pg 39.

God tests Abram a second time and again Abram's reaction is self-centred. *'What can you give me?'* But he believed the promise God gave him, and this was counted to him for righteousness (15:1-6).

The third test finds Abram still selfish and impatient (16:1-2). The result is the birth of Ishmael thus causing trouble and grief. Still God did not cast him off!

Ishmael was born because Abram did not wait on God's time: we too must be careful not to rush in before God's time. If we do, we can cause more trouble for ourselves, as Abram and Sarai did.

Stage two (conflict). Through his trials Abram comes to maturity (17:1-7) He falls face down (vs. 17) ready to give his all to the Lord. God had waited for Abram to die to himself. Now God gives him a further promise and changes his name to Abraham and Sarai's name to Sarah. Abraham then covenants with God and circumcises each male of his household. He pleads for Sodom and Gomorrah (ch. 18), showing his growing maturity and closeness to God.

Abraham is still not perfect, he risks Sarah's life again even after he has been told that she is to bear him the son promised by God. The Lord graciously protects Sarah and keeps her inviolate (ch. 20).

Finally Isaac is born; the fulfilment of God's promise gives Abraham joy and gladness and having this son given to him increases his maturity of character (21:1-4). He must have shared his story with Isaac, impressing upon him the wonder of God's dealings, and the great future that awaited their family.

From this point Abraham becomes a type of the Father sacrificing his only Son.

Stage three (contemplation): God tests Abraham again and this time Abraham is ready to give God everything. He says, *'Here I am'* (22:1). He has been brought to the place of full dependence upon God, not trusting in himself. This is the place to which the Lord would have all his saints come, because when this stage is reached then the glory of a task completed will not be taken to self but wholly given to God. It is in this place that God can trust us, his servants, to do his will without fail.

Abraham made two faith statements that proved he believed the promise of God that Isaac would be the father of many nations; that he would not die but live to give glory to God. In verse five he told his servants, *'The boy and I will come back to you.'* And in verse eight he said to Isaac, *'God himself will provide the lamb for the burnt offering, my son.'*

In the journey up Mt. Moriah and the drama enacted there we see an image of the Father (God) with his Son (Jesus). As Abraham climbs the hill and places his son on the altar we see an outstanding picture of Calvary. It was indeed a marvellous foreshadowing of the love of God for all mankind (John 3:16).

Offering Isaac on Mt. Moriah was the greatest trial of Abraham's life, but it was also the most wonderful victory. Abraham named the mountain Jehoveh-Jireh, *'The Lord will provide'* (Genesis 22:14). He believed God's promise for the future so he said to his servants, *'The boy and I will come back to you.'* What a man of faith he had become!

At the supreme moment of trial, just as Abraham was about to plunge the knife into his son the angel of the Lord called to him from heaven –

> *'Abraham! Abraham!' 'Here I am,' he replied. 'Do not lay a hand on the boy,' he said. 'Do not do anything to him. Now I know that you fear God, because you have not withheld from me your son, your only son'* (22:11-12).

Abraham's faith was vindicated and God provided a different sacrifice for him to offer there on the mountain.

God gave many more blessings once Abraham qualified for them and it is true that God must test us before he blesses us and we must continue to trust him through each time of testing. God tests us to see what is in our heart (Deuteronomy 8:2) and we are enlarged and made more mature under this kind of pressure (Psalm 4:1).

Abraham progressed from being a selfish individual intent upon preserving his own life, to a man who was willing to trust God completely, even to the extremity of being willing to give his son of promise, for whom he had waited so long. He trusted God so completely that he knew, even if he had to offer Isaac, somehow God would bring him back to life.

This type is given authority from the New Testament (Hebrews 11:17-19).

Isaac – A Type of Jesus, The Son of Promise

There are many parallels between the life of Isaac (Genesis chs. 21 & 22) and the life of Jesus (Galatians 4:23, 28-31).

Isaac was heir to the promise of a temporal kingdom in Canaan. Christ is heir to the kingdom of God and is now risen to the highest place at the right hand of God (Colossians 1:15-20). We, through Christ who is our heavenly Isaac, have access to our heavenly inheritance in God's kingdom (2 Corinthians 4:16-18; Ephesians 1:13-14).

A good and kind father, Abraham, prepared his beloved and innocent son, Isaac, to suffer death. God in reality gave his One and Only Son to suffer that we might live (John 3:16-17).

Isaac carried the wood on which he was later bound ready to be sacrificed. Christ carried the wooden cross to which he was nailed (19:17).

There was a God-appointed place for Isaac to be offered, and Christ knew on which mount he was to die. He had no doubt seen others crucified there many times.

We have the time of three days specified in each case. Isaac had a substitute die in his place; for Jesus, the three days ended in his resurrection (Luke 24:1-8).

God provided a ram for Isaac and Jesus is the lamb sacrificed for us. Both the ram and the lamb are associated with temple sacrifices.

Rebekah, Isaac's Bride – A Type of The Bride of Christ

The touching and romantic story of Isaac and Rebekah shows Abraham sending his servant Eliezer to seek out a bride for Isaac and the triumphant return and subsequent marriage are shown as part of God's plan (Genesis ch.24). The types in this love story are these:

Abraham, the father of Isaac, sending his servant to find a wife for his son, is a type of God the Father sending the Holy Spirit to find a bride for his Son, Jesus.

Eliezer, Abraham's trusted servant, being guided and directed by God to find a wife for Isaac, depicts the Holy Spirit seeking out the church, the perfect bride for Jesus.

Isaac, the son of promise eagerly awaiting his bride, is a type of Christ the Son preparing in his Father's house for his bride, the church.

Rebekah, the bride being adorned with the gifts provided by Abraham, projects a picture of the church being adorned with gifts by the Holy Spirit to make her ready for her husband, King Jesus.

Joseph – A Type of Jesus As Preserver, Provider, and Saviour

In Joseph we see a brilliant cameo of Jesus (Genesis ch.37 – ch.48).

There is no sin recorded in the Old Testament against Joseph's life, and Jesus was holy and without sin (Luke 1:35).

Joseph had two dreams, which kept him focussed on the will of God throughout his thirteen years of suffering. Jesus knew who he was from the prophecies of the Old Testament and these gave him perfect confidence to live out the will of God (John 5:30).

Joseph was sold by his brothers for 20 pieces of silver. Jesus was sold by Judas, one of his disciples, for 30 pieces of silver (Luke 22:1-6) and then crucified, because his own people clamoured for it (23:26-49).

Joseph was falsely accused and cast into prison. Jesus was falsely accused and died on the cross (Luke 23:44-46).

Joseph was finally freed from prison. Jesus rose from the dead on the third day (24:1-7).

Joseph was taken from prison and raised to the second highest position in the land. Jesus was raised from death to sit on the right hand of the Father in heaven (Acts 7:55-56).

Joseph provided for the people of Egypt and was instrumental in saving his family also from starvation. Jesus has made provision for our salvation by his death and resurrection (John 1:13-14; 1Timothy 3:16).

Joseph forgave his brothers after first testing their love and protection for Benjamin, to make sure they had changed. Jesus forgave those who killed him (Luke 23:34).

God allowed the trials in Joseph's life so that he could preserve his family many years later. He was only seventeen when he was sold into slavery and thirty when he was raised up to rule Egypt under Pharaoh (Genesis 41:46a). During this period God changed Joseph, partly through the things he suffered, but also through learning to manage Potiphar's household, and then later on through helping the jailer in the administration of the jail.

Consequently Joseph was changed from being a spoilt, favoured son of his indulgent and loving father Jacob, and became instead a strong and wise ruler and an adept administrator.

Sometimes when Christians are in trouble they keep humble, but then when they are lifted up to a position of trust they fail because of pride. Joseph did not make this mistake; he kept a good attitude all through his life.

Aaron, The Priests and Levites — A Type of Jesus As High Priest

In the priestly class we see mirrored the priesthood of Jesus (Exodus ch.29). The priests were to be consecrated, set apart for God, and the basis for their consecration was the blood of the sacrifice.

Aaron, the high priest representing Christ, is anointed before the slaying of the sacrifice. The other priests, representing us Christians as believer priests, are anointed after the sacrifice.

Aaron and his sons are anointed on the tip of the right ear, on the right thumb and on the big toe of the right foot. This anointing represents protection from sin through things we hear, sin through things we can touch, and sin through living in the wrong way (Exodus 29:19-21). John Gill makes this clear –

> The hands and fingers being the instruments of action, and the feet and toes of walking, show that the life and conversation of the priests of the Lord ought to be pure and holy, and so their antitype perfectly was; and whereas there is imperfection in all the actions, and even in the best righteousness of the saints, and their walk and conversation is not without sin, they have need to have them sprinkled with, and their conversation garments washed and made white in the blood of the Lamb. [20]

Jesus is our great High Priest who understands our weaknesses (Hebrews 4:14-16).

We as believers are a holy priesthood (1 Peter 2:5), but all Christians do not exercise the same ministry. Much depends upon our calling and our gifts and also on the depth of our relationship with Jesus. Our union with the Lord is one thing, but how close is our communion with him? Our standing in Christ is safe in the heavenlies, but what is the present state of our walk with the Lord?

---

[20] Gill, John. *Exposition of the Entire Bible;* E Sword; *in loc.*

Our relationship with God is one thing, but how are we serving him? We can complete the will of God for our life through the power of God and the refining of the Holy Spirit, but we need to be aware that we too have a responsibility (Philippians 2:12-13).

Moses – A Type of Jesus The Mediator Between God and Man

Moses shows us in type the Lord Jesus as Mediator for his people, and also as Prophet, Priest and King (Numbers 14:1-23; 1Timothy 2:5).

There is a Jewish tradition that Moses wrote the book of Job while he was in the desert. If that is so he had a very good understanding of the role of intercessor (Job 9:33-34; 16:19-21).

After challenging all the gods of Egypt, by means of the plagues, and overcoming them with God's power, Moses led the children of Israel through the Passover and the final exodus. His greatest moment of triumph was when he led the people on dry land through the Red Sea (Exodus 14: 19-31; 15:1-18).

From there on the people began to grumble and complain, first at Marah where they found bitter water (15:23-25), then in the Desert of Sin where God rained down quail in the evening and manna in the morning (Exodus ch.16; Numbers 11:31-34). After this, water came from the rock at Horeb when Moses cried out to the Lord (Exodus 17:4-7).

When Moses came down from the mountain with the Ten Commandments chiseled in stone, he was horrified to see that the children of Israel, with Aaron's help, had made themselves a golden calf. In anger Moses broke the tablets of stone. The next day he said to the people, '*I will go up to the Lord; perhaps I can make atonement for your sin*' (32:30).

There he made a sublime statement, offering himself in place of the people, '*Oh, what a great sin these people have committed! They have made themselves gods of gold. But now please forgive their sin – but if not, then blot me out of the book you have written*'

(32:31). Here Moses showed himself a true mediator between his people and God.

He showed himself mediator again when the twelve spies returned from Canaan (Numbers 14:1-23), and after the rebellion of Korah (16:1-40), and then after the people grumbled again *'the very next day'* (16:41-50).

Moses showed himself as a mediator by these signs:

- He was willing to pray and plead for the people (Exodus 15:25; 32:31-32) Numbers 14:11-19).
- He sought the favour of God for the people (Numbers 14:13-16).
- He did not consider his own advancement (Exodus 32:32).
- He instructed Aaron to make atonement for the people (Leviticus 9:7).
- He was willing to give his life for the people (Exodus 32:32).

Moses was willing to die for his people and even to be blotted out of God's book of life to save them from the wrath of God. In this he showed himself a true type of Christ who died that we might live, and gave himself a ransom for many. Moses offered himself for his own people, but Christ died for all people (1Timothy 2:5-6; Hebrews 4:14-16; 7:24-25).

Moses also typified Christ as Prophet, Priest and King.

Moses as Prophet:

A Prophet speaks to the people and gives them a message from God; Moses was the law giver, and revealed God's mind to the people. Jesus as a prophet gave his commands and laid out his manifesto for the kingdom of God (Matthew chs. 6 & 7). He also revealed God to us who believe; he came to show us our God is full of love, mercy, grace and truth.

Moses as Priest:

The priest speaks to God in prayer on behalf of the people! Moses was commanded by God to ratify the Covenant between God and the Israelites by sprinkling blood (Exodus 24:8). Jesus shed his blood and no-one can come to God except through his atoning work (John 14:6).

In his intercessory ministry Moses, through his prayers, obtained blessings for the Israelites and at other times turned the wrath of God away from them. Jesus is our great High Priest interceding for us in the heavenlies, protecting us and blessing us with all spiritual blessings (Hebrews 7:25-28; Ephesians 1:3).

Moses as Leader/King.

Moses was divinely appointed as the ruler and the leader of the Israelites; Jesus is the head of his church and will one day reign as King of kings and Lord of lords (Revelation 19:11-16).

Chapter Seven:

Types of Christ

In this chapter we continue to explore the pictures of Christ abounding in the Old Testament. They reveal Christ in many different ways, each one helping us to plumb further depths of either his character or his ministry

Joshua — A Type of Jesus The Captain of Our Salvation

The leadership of Joshua marks the beginning of a new era in the life of the children of Israel. Joshua is given God's promise of great strength: God will be with him wherever he goes (Joshua 1:9). When the people of Israel get to Jericho the Lord appears to Joshua as Commander of the army of the Lord (5:13-15). Joshua becomes a type of Jesus as the true Captain of our salvation (Hebrews 2:10 KJV). Jesus is the one with all authority in heaven and in earth (Matthew 28:18-20).

Boaz — A Type of Christ The Kinsman Redeemer

In the beautiful love story of Ruth and Boaz we see the over-ruling hand of God, working out his purposes. Ruth is a remarkable lady, loving and kind, and with the soul of a poet (Ruth 1:16-17). She was chosen by God to be an ancestor of Jesus. Her son, Obed, became the grandfather of David from whose line the Messiah would come.

The story teaches redemption in type. Boaz represents Christ and Ruth represents the church (ch.4). We, the church, are redeemed and brought back from the enemy even as in the story Ruth is redeemed (Ephesians 5:1-2; Titus 2:11-14; 1 Peter 1:18-19).

Samuel – A Type of Christ

Samuel represents Christ in many ways. He was a son of promise; Hannah was promised a son after her agonised prayer (1 Samuel 1:17). Jesus was the Son promised to Mary through the word of the angel Gabriel (Luke 1:31-33).

Samuel was dedicated to the Lord from a young age. Hannah said, *'So now I give him to the Lord. For his whole life he will be given over to the Lord.'* (1 Samuel 1:27-28; 2:1-11). Jesus was the Lord's from his birth (Luke 1: 35, 2:23-24).

From his youth Samuel showed a strong and balanced character, he was obedient and truthful, and respected authority (1 Samuel ch 3). Jesus grew and became strong, he was filled with wisdom and the grace of God was on him (Luke 1:40). He was and is the way the truth and the life (John 14:6).

Samuel showed zeal in leading people to repentance (1 Samuel 7:3). It was prophesied of Jesus, *'Zeal for your house consumes me'* (Psalm 69:9), and he showed this zeal when he drove the money changers from the temple (John 2:13-17).

Samuel had no fear of man but as a judge he ruled diligently in the fear of God (1 Samuel 7:15-17; 12:1-5). Jesus had no fear of man or of any circumstance, he was fearless in his attacks on the scribes and Pharisees (Matthew ch. 23); he was unafraid in the teeth of the storm (Luke 8:22-25) and he stood fearlessly before his accusers (Lu 22:63-23:24). Now he has all authority, given to him by God (Matthew 28:18).

Samuel sought divine direction (1 Samuel 7:7-13; 8:19-22). Jesus also sought God's will in all things: he would not do or say anything without God's direction (John 12:49-50).

God did not allow one word spoken by Samuel to fall to the ground (1 Samuel 3:19). Jesus is the Word of God which shall never pass away (Luke 21:33).

Jonah – The Death, Burial, and Resurrection of Christ

The book of Jonah is the story of a missionary who tried to evade the task given him by God, to warn the people of Nineveh of their impending doom (Jonah ch.1). In that story God shows his mercy toward those who do not know him and his willingness that all should be given the opportunity to be rescued from sin and eternal death (2 Peter 3:9). In type he showed the merciful nature of Christ Jesus that was to be mirrored in his earthly ministry (Matthew 9:27-37).

In Jonah we see Christ in his death and resurrection. Jesus himself said this was the only sign that would be given to the scribes and Pharisees. As Jonah was three days and three nights in the belly of the great fish so Jesus was to rise on the third day after his crucifixion (Matthew 12:38-40; Luke 11:29-32).

David – A Type of Jesus as Shepherd, Ruler, and King

To David the Messiah to come was to be the King of Zion (Psalm 2 and 24). David was a man of his times, beginning his working life as a shepherd but becoming in time a great warrior king. Though in many ways he was a *'man after God's own heart'* he was also a man of blood. He had to fight many battles to weld Israel and Judah into one kingdom and to overcome all his enemies so that Solomon, his son, could in turn have a peaceful reign. David was also *'the sweet singer of Israel'*. He had many redeeming qualities and showed a remarkable spiritual insight. He was a poetic visionary who gave us many Messianic prophecies throughout his Psalms (Psalm 2; 16; 22; 23; 24; 110). He loved the Word of God (119:97-104) and he knew how to encourage himself in the Lord (1 Samuel 30:6; Psalm 143:5-10). He was a patient man; he refused to touch the Lord's anointed but waited for God's timing to bring him the crown (1 Samuel chs.24 & 26). He showed mercy to his enemies, Mephibosheth (2 Samuel ch.9), Absalom (13:39) and Shimei (19:23) He was honourable; when his three mighty men risked their lives to get him water from the well near the gate of Bethlehem, he refused to drink it but poured it out before the Lord (23:15-17).

It is easy to imagine David in his early days, playing on his harp while he tended the sheep for his father, meditating on God and developing his spiritual life. No doubt his shepherd psalm (Psalm 23) would have come to him while he meditated on the goodness and mercy of God. He trained for many hours with his sling shot, and this expertise would have stood him in good stead when the lion and then the bear came to devastate his flock of sheep.

By the time David faced Goliath he knew what he was capable of, he was prepared, and he had faith in God to help him in his hour of need. His rise to leadership after this was assured until Saul became jealous of his popularity.

Then David had to flee into the desert but even this set back was used by God – *'All those who were in distress or in debt or discontented gathered around him, and he became their leader'* (1 Samuel 22:2). Consolidating hundreds of these men into an army proved David's leadership capabilities and prepared him for the kingship God had promised him.

Jesus is our leader and our shepherd, as he said in the gospel of John, *'The thief comes only to steal and to kill and destroy; I have come that they may have life, and have it to the full. I am the good shepherd. The good shepherd lays down his life for his sheep'* (John 10:10-11).

Finally at the age of thirty David was crowned:

> *When all of the elders of Israel had come to King David at Hebron, the king made a compact with them at Hebron before the Lord, and they anointed David king over Israel. David was thirty years old when he became king, and he reigned forty years. In Hebron he reigned over Judah seven years and six months, and in Jerusalem he reigned over all Israel and Judah thirty three years* (2 Samuel 5:3-5).

Jesus will one day be crowned King of kings and all will bow the knee before him:

> *The Lord says to my Lord; 'Sit at my right hand until I make your enemies a footstool for your feet.' The Lord will extend your mighty sceptre from Zion; you will rule in the midst of your enemies* (Psalm 110:1-2).

Solomon – The Wisdom of The Saviour

Solomon was given his wisdom by God in answer to his prayer (1 Kings 3:7-15), but his wisdom though great was limited. By contrast, in Christ there are hidden all the treasures of wisdom and knowledge (Proverbs 8; Colossians 2:2-3). Paul urged the Colossians, and in turn all the saints down through the gospel age, to be encouraged in heart and united in love to reach complete wisdom and understanding. Christ has all the wisdom we could ever need. In James we are encouraged again to seek the wisdom of God. As we seek his wisdom we will not be denied for God gives generously without finding fault (James 1:5).

Jeremiah – A Type of Christ

Jeremiah was like Christ in many ways. He not only revealed Christ in his prophecies but he reflected Christ in his personality. His name Jeremiah means 'he shall exalt Jehovah'. His whole life was spent in the endeavour to promote God's glory. Jesus also came to promote God's glory. As he prayed to his Father, '*I have brought you glory on earth by completing the work you gave me to do*' (John 17:4).

Dr. Moorehead expresses Jeremiah's likeness to Christ so well –

> One cannot but see in Jeremiah something of the Spirit of Christ. Indeed, it is not too much to say that on a small scale, that Life which is above all other lives is reproduced in this prophet. Jeremiah's love for his people, his anxiety to do them good and naught but good, his tears at the defeat of his efforts to reclaim them, and the hopefulness with which he looks forward to their final recovery and blessing are but a

dim reflection of what was perfect in the heart of the Lord Jesus. Grace and the Spirit of God will make anyone like Christ.[21]

Jeremiah, named the weeping prophet, was a man of sorrows who grieved for his people. He is a great example to us to be faithful even though we may see little fruit for our labours. In Jeremiah's prophetic utterances we see Jesus as the Fountain of Living Water (Jeremiah 2:13; 17:13 cp. John 4:13-14; 7:37-39); the Great Physician (Jeremiah 8:22; Matthew 4:23-24; Acts 10:38); the Good Shepherd (Jeremiah 23:3; 31:10; Psalm 23; John 10:1-11); the Righteous Branch (Jeremiah 23:5-6; Isaiah 11:1); the Lord Our Righteousness (Jeremiah 23:6; Romans 5:18; 2Corinthians 5:17,21); The Redeemer (Jeremiah 50:34; Ephesians 1:7; Colossians 1:13-14), and Christ pictured in David the king (Jeremiah 30:9; Matthew 1:17; 20:29-30; Acts 2:25-36).

Jeremiah wept over Jerusalem as he foretold the destruction of the city by the Chaldeans; Jesus also wept over Jerusalem as he predicted its future destruction by the Romans. This prophecy Jesus gave came true with terrible finality in AD 70 (Luke 21: 20-24).

Several shadows of the cross can be traced in Lamentations –

> *Is it nothing to you, all you who pass by? Look around and see. Is any suffering like my suffering that was inflicted on me, that the Lord brought on me in the day of his fierce anger* (Lamentations 1:12).

> *All who pass your way clap their hands at you; they scoff and shake their heads ... All your enemies open their mouths wide against you; they scoff and gnash their teeth* (Lamentations 2:15a &16a; cp. Matthew 27:39-40).

---

[21] Moorehead , W. G. (1836-1914); A United Presbyterian minister; An editor of the *Scofield Reference Bible* and a conservative and evangelical theological writer and teacher.

> *Even when I call out or cry for help, he shuts out my prayer* (Lamentations 3:8; cp. Matthew 27 46)
>
> *I became the laughing stock of all my people* (Lamentations 3:14a).
>
> *I remember my affliction and my wandering, the bitterness and the gall* (3:19; cp. Psalm 69: 21; Matthew 27:48).
>
> *Let him offer his cheek to one who would strike him and let him be filled with disgrace* (Lamentations 3:30; cp. Isaiah 50:6; Psalm 69:20).
>
> *But it happened because of the sins of her prophets and the iniquities of her priests, who shed within her the righteous blood* (Lamentations 4:13; cp. Acts 3:13- 15, 1 Peter 3:18).

In the midst of apostasy, judgment and disaster, Jeremiah set his face, as Jesus did later, 'steadfastly toward Jerusalem.' As Jesus was broken hearted so Jeremiah suffered the same agony –

> *My heart! My heart! I writhe in pain! The walls of my heart will break! My heart groans within me; I cannot keep it still* (Jeremiah 4:19 free translation).

Elijah — A Type of John The Baptist and of Christ

Elijah called Israel to repentance; he showed the power of God; and he wrought eight miracles during his life. He prophesied drought in Israel (1 Kings 17:1); he prophesied that the widow of Zarephath's meal and oil would not fail until the famine was over (17:7-16), and he raised the son of the same widow to life again (17:17-24). He commanded the elements by calling down fire from heaven on the altar he had built on Mt Carmel (1 Kings 18:16-40), then prayed successfully for the three year drought to end (18:41-45). After being fed by the angel in Beersheba he fasted 40 days and 40 nights on his journey to Horeb (19:8-9). He called down fire from heaven on two captains of king Ahaziah and their fifty soldiers (2 Kings 1:1-15). At the end of his life he went over

Jordan dry shod and then was caught up to heaven in a whirlwind (2 Kings 2:1-12).

Elijah pointed the way back to God as John the Baptist would do in his day (Luke 3:1-18). Jesus said John was the Elijah who was to come (Malachi 4:5-6; Matthew 17:10-13).

In his control of the forces of nature Elijah foreshadowed some of the miracles Jesus wrought. In turning water into wine (John 2:1-11), feeding the five thousand (6:1-15), walking on water; controlling the winds and the waves (6:15-24), healing the sick (Matthew 8:14-17), and raising the dead (John ch.11), Jesus showed his great power over his creation and thus proved his claim to be the Messiah.

Elisha – A Type of The Holy Spirit.

Elisha had a double portion of the spirit of Elijah and therefore wrought 16 miracles; he divided the waters of Jordan (2 Kings 2:14); he healed the waters of Jericho (2:19-22); he caused bears to maul the delinquent youths (2:23-25); he caused water to flow in the desert of Edom (3:15-20); he multiplied the widow's cruse of oil (4:1-7); he prophesied that the Shunamite woman would have a son (4:15-17) and later he restored her son to life (4:18-37); he caused the pot of poison to be harmless (4:38-41); he multiplied twenty barley loaves to feed a hundred men (4:42-44); he healed Naaman of leprosy (ch.5); he prophesied Gehazi would have leprosy in Naaman's place as he sought to gain from the miracle of healing (5:19-27); he caused an axe head to float (6:1-7); he prayed for his servant's eyes to be opened so he could see God's chariots of fire (6:17); then struck the Arameans with blindness (6:8-23); he correctly prophesied the time the siege would be lifted from Samaria (6:24-33 & ch.7); and after his death his bones brought a man back to life (13:20-21).

He is considered to be a type of the Holy Spirit (John 7:37-39) because he continued the work of Elijah after he was caught up to heaven, even as the Holy Spirit continued the work of Jesus after his ascension.

In multiplying the bread for the hundred, in restoring the Shunamite woman's son to life, and in healing Naaman of leprosy, he foreshadowed three types of miracles wrought by Christ in his ministry.

Daniel – A Type of Christ

Daniel was a man loved by God and respected by all who knew him (Daniel 6:25-28). He was filled with the Spirit of wisdom (1:17; 5:13-14), and he was a man of prevailing prayer (6:10-11; 9:4-23) and was given knowledge of what the future held. In these ways he represents Christ who was all these things and more. Daniel was a prophet with whom God shared much, and his book has similar symbols to the book of *Revelation,* so that it is a good idea to study them together (Daniel 7:1-14; cp. Revelation 1:12-18; 13:5-6; 19:19-21).

Daniel was privileged to see a vision of the second coming of Christ:

> *In my vision at night I looked, and there before me was one like a son of man, coming with the clouds of heaven. He approached the Ancient of Days and was led into his presence. He was given authority, glory and sovereign power; all peoples and nations and men of every language worshiped him. His dominion is an everlasting dominion that will not pass away, and his kingdom is one that will never be destroyed* (7:13-14).

Chapter Eight:

Saviour, Shepherd and Sovereign

A trilogy of Messianic Psalms

Jesus, Our Suffering Saviour

Jesus' cry of agony '*My God, my God, why have you forsaken me?*' recorded in Psalm 22:1 and also in Matthew 27:46 must have amazed all the Jewish men standing around the cross. They would have known this psalm by heart, and indeed all of the psalms, for they learned them by rote at their village school.

The chief priests, the teachers of the law, and the elders who had just finished mocking and jeering Jesus as he hung on the cross, should have been convicted and fearful, remembering that some of the words they had been speaking (Matthew 27:43) were actually part of this psalm –

> *He trusts in the Lord; let the Lord rescue him. Let him deliver him, since he delights in him* (Psalm 22:8).

The description of the crucifixion and its effect on the physical body – the piercing of the hands and feet, the bones out of joint, and the thirst (Psalm 22:14-17) these were all fulfilled by Jesus' death and recorded in John 19.

> *I am poured out like water, and all my bones are out of joint. My heart has turned to wax; it has melted away within me* (Psalm 22:14).

This indicates a broken heart which was shown to be true by the fact that blood and water flowed from his side when the Roman soldier speared him to make sure he was dead (John 19:34).

> *They divided my garments among them and cast lots for my clothing* (Psalm 22:18).

One thousand years before Jesus died on the cross, David saw this all in a vision and predicted it accurately.

His suffering was spiritual as well as physical:

The physical suffering of Jesus must have been terrible, but we can never know nor understand what incredible *spiritual* suffering he endured. Christ had never known a moment without his Father's fellowship. This was a close and beautiful union which enabled him to say, *'Anyone who has seen me has seen the Father'* (Jn 14:9b) and, *'the words I say to you are not just my own. Rather it is the Father, living in me, who is doing his work'* (10b).

When that wonderful relationship was cut off suddenly, I'm sure this must have been a shock to Jesus. Even though he knew it had to happen, he may have had no previous understanding of just what a soul-wrenching agony it would prove to be.

Jesus knew this Psalm, not only by heart but also both from his Jewish upbringing and from his diligent searching of the Old Testament. Though he only had the strength to quote the first few words, the rest of the Psalm must have also been in his mind, so he knew that even though his Father had turned his back for a moment, and that Satan thought he had won the victory, it was God the Father who had everything under control!

Yes, Satan was there at the cross:

> *Many bulls surround me; strong bulls of Bashan encircle me. Roaring lions tearing their prey open their mouths wide against me* (Psalm 22:12-13).

But despite Satan's seeming victory, Jesus knew that in three days his Father would keep his promise and that he would rise again from the tomb, never again to suffer the humiliation or the agony of the cross. Because he knew these things, he was able to pray a last trusting prayer *'Father into your hands I commend my spirit'* (Luke 23:46). This prayer was made by Jewish children each night before they went to sleep, and it shows the unshakeable trust Jesus had in the promise-keeping power of his Father.

Jesus knew that he would be vindicated for the Psalm goes on -

> *From you comes the theme of my praise in the great assembly; before those who fear you will I fulfil my vows. The poor will eat and be satisfied; they who seek the Lord will praise him – may your hearts live forever! All the ends of the earth will remember and turn to the Lord, and all the families of the nations will bow down before him, for dominion belongs to the Lord and he rules over the nations. All the rich of the earth will feast and worship; all who go down to the dust will kneel before him—those who cannot keep themselves alive. Posterity will serve him; future generations will be told about the Lord. They will proclaim his righteousness to a people yet unborn – for he has done it* (Psalm 22: 25-31).

Jesus knew that he would fulfil his vows; that future generations would praise him; that the poor would be satisfied; that nations would bow down before him; that future generations would be told about him; that his righteousness would be proclaimed.

For he has done it! He has completed his task!

He has not suffered in vain – we are one of those future generations that praise and thank him for his sacrifice, and we know that one day every knee will bow and every tongue confess that he is Lord!

Jesus, Our Supporting Shepherd

Jesus is our shepherd and we should learn to know his voice for we are the sheep of his pasture (Psalm 23:1),

The shepherd cares for his flock. Still in some parts of the Middle -East today you can see shepherds taking care of their flocks. In Bible days, shepherds would gather together and mingle their flocks behind a barrier as a protection against predators. When morning came the shepherds would go to different points of the compass and call their sheep. Knowing their master's voice the sheep would come quickly to the side of their shepherd, thus separating the flock without any trouble at all.

> *...The sheep listen to his voice. He calls his own sheep by name and leads them out. When he has brought out all his own, he goes on ahead of them, and his sheep follow him because they know his voice* (John 10: 3-4).

A lone shepherd out on the hillside at night would lay himself down in the doorway of the thorny shelter he had created for his sheep. In this way he would know if any of his flock strayed outside the safety he had provided. This is what Jesus meant when he referred to the gate of the sheepfold, He is the one who provides eternal security for us and opens the way for us to know God's voice.

> *I am the gate; whoever enters in through me will be saved, He will come in and go out, and find pasture* (John 10:9

He provides safe water and feed for them (Psalm 23:2). Sheep will not drink from running water as they know instinctively that it is dangerous for them. If they were to fall in the weight of their wool would drown them. The shepherd must provide quiet water by constructing a pool apart from the flowing stream. There the sheep can drink without fear. The shepherd will look also for lush green pastures where the sheep can graze in peace.

When we read and meditate on his Word and listen to his voice Jesus leads us and guides us into green pastures and beside still waters. These are spiritual food and the life giving water of God which he gives to us so freely. We find instructions to desire this Word –

> *When your words came, I ate them (I absorbed them into my very being); they were my joy and my heart's delight, for I bear your name, O Lord God Almighty* (Jeremiah 15:16). *Let the word of Christ dwell in you richly...* (Colossians 3:16a).

Jesus restores our soul (23:3) as we trust and obey him. He replenishes our inner being; he fills us to overflowing with his goodness and he guides us into his righteous paths for his name's sake. Slowly but surely as we rest in him, he changes us and transforms us into his image.

> *And we, who with unveiled faces all reflect the Lord's glory, are being transformed into his likeness with ever increasing glory, which comes from the Lord who is the Spirit* (2 Corinthians 3:18).

Long ago, when a silversmith was refining silver, he placed it into the crucible and subjected it to intense heat. One came along and saw what he was doing and asked him 'How do you know when the silver is completely pure?' He said, 'That is simple, when I can see my perfect reflection in it I know it is pure.' As we read in Proverbs. *Remove dross from the silver, and out comes material for the silversmith* (Proverbs 25:4).

Jesus is our silversmith and we are made pure by his righteousness. Though sometimes the trials we go through may seem grievous; though sometimes we may feel we are called to endure fire, we know that he is with us and, *all things work together for good to them that love him and are called according to his purpose* (Romans 8:28).

He is with us always and we are comforted (Psalm 23:4), through death experiences and grief experiences. We need not fear any evil for he is watching over us, even when we do not feel his presence. The rod the shepherd carried was a cudgel for beating off robbers and wild animals. The staff had a hook on it to rescue the lambs that wandered away from the flock and fell over rocky precipices. Knowing our Shepherd has our safety and rescue in hand comforts us. He will protect us from the evil one and bring us at last into his presence.

He prepares a table before us in the presence of our enemies (23:5), he feeds us spiritually even when we are under attack from our enemy, Satan, and strengthens us to bear the temptations and to come through the battles victoriously. He anoints us for service, and we are filled with joy.

He grants us his goodness (23:6), his own righteousness, his love, and his mercy for our sins so that one day we will be able to dwell with him forever.

Jesus, Our Supreme Sovereign

Jesus, our Supreme Sovereign, is now reigning in heaven, seated at the right hand of the Father. He is preparing to return to receive the homage he deserves. When that day comes every knee will bow and every person will declare him to be King of kings and Lord of lords, for the earth is his and everything in it belongs to him (Psalm 24:1).

In our day Christian people tend to regard Jesus as Bridegroom rather than Sovereign Lord. In Bible days a king had absolute power of life and death over his people. It behoves us to remember that our King is such a king and to walk carefully before him in obedience. There are too many today who have no fear of God.

> *The fear* (solemn respect), *of the Lord is the beginning of wisdom and all who follow his precepts have good understanding. To him belongs eternal praise* (Psalm 111:10).

We who would be his servants must heed the admonition of this Psalm:

> '*Who may ascend the hill of the Lord? Who may stand in his holy place? He who has clean hands and a pure heart, who does not lift up his soul to an idol or swear by what is false* (Psalm 24:3-4).

We must have clean hands and a pure heart, there should be no idols in our life; nothing should come before our Saviour! If we purify ourselves and remain rooted in his love then we will receive his blessing and vindication (24:5).

In that great day when he comes in the clouds with his angelic hosts (Matthew 24:30-31), he will receive the homage he deserves as our supreme Sovereign and Lord. Every knee will bow and every tongue will confess that he is Lord of all!

> *Lift up your heads, O you gates; be lifted up, you ancient doors, that the King of glory may come in. Who is this King of glory? The Lord strong and mighty, the Lord mighty in battle* (24:7-8)

Chapter Nine:

Christ in Isaiah

The book of Isaiah is full of poetic imagery. It is called the Bible in miniature as it has sixty-six chapters and is divided into two parts. The Bible itself having sixty-six books and being divided into the Old and New Testaments. Isaiah was a fervent prophet, a skilful poet, and part of the aristocracy of Israel. He presents in his writings the prophetic story of the Messiah from before the present creation on into eternity. He also brings out the refreshing, restoring power of God in all his fullness.

Many times in Scripture the Lord is likened to springs of water (Jeremiah 2:13; 17:13; John 7:38). Isaiah also uses springs of water, rivers, and wells of water to represent God and his ability to restore fruitfulness to the land and its people. The Lord promises he will satisfy the thirsty soul and bring fruitfulness to lives that have been a desert of sin and sorrow (Isaiah 41:17-18).

Indeed Isaiah, in one of his Messianic promises, claims a time of favour will come when the Messiah will be a covenant for the people, restoring them, delivering them and leading them beside streams of living water (49:8-10).

Then again the Lord promises his people he will satisfy them, strengthening them so they will be like a well-watered garden, like a spring whose waters never fail. Living water comes from God himself to bring nourishment to the souls and feelings and emotions of people in need (58:11-12).

In chapter twelve Isaiah composes a glorious song about the fact that it is the Lord who will be the Saviour, that he is the one to bring us wholeness. We will be thirsty no longer for he will provide for us deep wells of the water of life.

> *'Surely God is my salvation; I will trust and not be afraid. The Lord, the Lord is my strength and my song; he has become my salvation.' With joy you will draw water from the wells of salvation. In that day you will say; 'Give thanks to the Lord, call on his name; make known among the nations what he has done, and proclaim that his name is exalted for he has done glorious things; let this be known to all the world.'* (12:2-5)

Isaiah's prophecies are so exact that it seems to us that he actually sees the scenes he describes and Barnes agrees –

> The representation of future scenes was made known to the prophets by visions. This idea ... intimates that in a dream, and in the state of prophetic ecstasy, events were made known to them, not by words, but by causing the scene to pass before their mind or their mental visions, as if they saw it. Thus the entire series of the prophecies of Isaiah is described as a vision in Isaiah 1:1 and 2 Chronicles 32:32.[22]

The Messiah is the Mighty God

As Isaiah sought the Lord earnestly he saw a vision of Jesus, surrounded by the supernal splendour that was his before he freely laid it aside to accomplish our salvation When he saw this vision Isaiah's whole heart and soul cried out to God to let him be his messenger. Immediately an angel touched his lips with a live coal from the altar and he was given a prophetic gift and a divine revelation of the Messiah who was to come. Over the years of his prophetic ministry Isaiah saw the life and death of the Messiah with amazing clarity (6:1-8).

In John's gospel we see a confirmation that the glorious vision given to Isaiah was indeed Jesus with the heavenly host. *Isaiah (said this) because he saw Jesus' glory and spoke about him* (John 12:41)

---

[22] Barnes, Albert; *Isaiah*; Volume One Pg. 47

In the paragraphs following we have the many prophecies Isaiah gave to us; all were fulfilled in the life of Jesus of Nazareth. Some we have already covered in this book, but we will repeat them as they show the remarkable number of prophecies given to Isaiah concerning the Messiah.

The Messiah will come

John the Baptist was chosen to be the one to announce to the world that the Messiah was come. He said, *'Behold the Lamb of God who takes away the sin of the world'* (John 1:29). Isaiah saw there was to be a herald to prepare the way –

> *A voice of one calling in the desert prepare the way for the Lord; make straight in the wilderness a highway for our God. Every valley shall be raised up, every mountain and hill made low; the rough ground shall become level, the rugged places a plain. And the glory of the Lord will be revealed, and all mankind together will see it. For the mouth of the Lord has spoken* (Isaiah 40: 3-5)

He will be born of a virgin

With his glorious baptism of fire Isaiah was given the commission to speak for the Lord and he went on to give prophecy after prophecy about the coming Saviour. One was that he would be born of a virgin, that he would somehow be *'God with us'*, dwelling here on the earth (Luke 1:26-38).

> *Therefore the Lord himself will give you a sign; the virgin will be with child and will give birth to a son, and will call him Immanuel* (Isaiah 7:14).

He will have a dual nature

This Saviour would be both Almighty God and yet also Prince of Peace, ruling with justice a kingdom that would last forever. He would also be fully human, a mystery belonging only to God. With our finite understanding we cannot fathom how God was able to fuse the divine and human natures into one small helpless baby.

However we know that with God all things are possible, whatever he decrees will be done (Luke 1:31-33).

> *For unto us a child is born, to us a son is given, and the government will be upon his shoulders. And he will be called Wonderful, Counselor, Mighty God, Everlasting Father, Prince of Peace. Of the increase of his government and peace there will be no end. He will reign on David's throne and over his kingdom, establishing and upholding it with justice and righteousness from that time on and forever. The zeal of the Lord Almighty will accomplish this* (Isaiah 9:6-7).

He will have a lowly beginning

This Saviour, coming from a poor and obscure family, though hidden royalty, would be descended from Jesse (Isaiah 11:10), then later according to promise, through Jesse's son, king David (Isaiah 11:10), and he would have great wisdom and understanding (Luke 2:52).

> *A shoot will come up from the stump of Jesse; from his roots a Branch will bear fruit. The Spirit of the Lord will rest on him – the Spirit of wisdom and of understanding, the Spirit of counsel and of power, the Spirit of knowledge and of the fear of the Lord – and he will delight in the fear of the Lord,.* (Isaiah 11:1-3a; see also 53:2).

He will minister in Galilee

Isaiah promises that those who walk in darkness would see a great light and those living in the shadow of spiritual death would gain revelation and understanding and so be filled with great joy (Luke 4:14-15).

> *In the future he will honour Galilee of the Gentiles, by the way of the sea, along the Jordan* (Isaiah 9:1b)

He will minister also to the Gentiles

How wonderful is our God, from the very beginning he planned that his children would come from every nation under heaven (Luke 7:1-10).

> *I will also make you a light for the Gentiles, that you may bring my salvation to the ends of the earth* (Isaiah 49:6b; see also 9:2-3; 42:6).

He will be the servant of the Lord

Through his prophet God promised that he would delight in his servant; His servant would not suffer discouragement, he would be faithful and be a covenant to the people of Israel. Through his servant, our Saviour, God would display his splendour, and make him a light also to the Gentiles, and a Saviour to all peoples (Isaiah 42:1-7; 49:1-7; 50:4-11; Philippians 2:6-10).

> *Listen to me, you islands; hear this, you distant nations. Before I was born the Lord called me; from my birth he has made mention of my name. He made my mouth like a sharpened sword, in the shadow of his hand he hid me; he made me into a polished arrow, and concealed me in his quiver. He said to me, 'You are my servant, Israel in whom I will display my splendour'* (Isaiah 49:1-3)

He will use parables

In chapter five Isaiah uses the parable method to speak to the people and this parable of his is reminiscent of one that Jesus told (cp. Isaiah 5:1-7 with Matthew 21:33-46). Jesus too would later use the parable method to speak to Israel for the same reasons given by Isaiah.

> *He said, 'Go and tell this people; Be ever hearing, but never understanding; be ever seeing, but never perceiving. Make the heart of this people calloused; make their ears dull and close their eyes. Otherwise they might see with their eyes, hear with their ears, understand with their hearts, and turn and be healed.'* (Isaiah 6:9-10).

He will establish an everlasting covenant

Our Saviour came to bring us the new covenant, ratified by his own blood. The old covenant with its sacrifices is forever done away. Now we have free access to the Father through the blood of Jesus (Hebrews 9:15). Isaiah knew of the promise to David –

> *Give ear and come to me; hear me, that your soul may live. I will make an everlasting covenant with you, my faithful love promised to David* (Isaiah 55:3).

He will bring freedom to the captives

Jesus came to heal the sick, to raise the dead, and to open blind eyes, these were in part his credentials, proof that he came from God, that he was the long awaited Messiah.

> *The Spirit of the Sovereign Lord is on me, because the Lord has anointed me to preach good news to the poor. He has sent me to bind up the broken hearted, to proclaim freedom for the captives and release from darkness for the prisoners, to proclaim the year of the Lord's favour and the day of the vengeance of our God, to comfort all who mourn–* (Isaiah 61:1-2; see also 3-11)

He will be despised and rejected

Though his disciples loved him and the common people heard him gladly (Mark 12:37b) Jesus was hated by those in authority because he threatened their way of life and exposed their sin (Matthew 27:41-43).

> *He was despised and rejected by men, a man of sorrows, and familiar with suffering.. Like one from whom men hide their faces he was despised, and we esteemed him not* (Isaiah 53:3).

He will not be particularly outstanding

Jesus during his three years of earthly ministry looked just like any other Jewish young man of around thirty years of age, he was not especially handsome in his appearance.

He had no beauty or majesty to attract us to him, nothing in his appearance that we should desire him (53:2b)

He will be disfigured

Isaiah saw in the spirit that the Messiah would be whipped with a Roman whip with its lethal pieces of sharpened bone which could literally tear the flesh from a man (John 19:1-3).

Just as there were many who were appalled at him – his appearance was so disfigured beyond that of any man and his form marred beyond human likeness– (Isaiah 52:14).

He will be pierced and crushed

When the soldiers went to break Jesus legs they found he was already dead. To make sure of his death they pierced his side and blood and water flowed out, proving his heart was broken for all mankind (John 19:32-35).

But he was pierced for our transgressions he was crushed for our iniquities; the punishment that brought us peace was upon him, and by his wounds we are healed (Isaiah 53:5)

He will make no complaint

Jesus was patient in his suffering and made no complaint when they whipped him, or when they nailed him to the cross. Rather he forgave his enemies (Luke 23:34).

He was oppressed and afflicted, yet he did not open his mouth: he was led like a lamb to the slaughter, and as a sheep before her shearers is silent, so he did not open his mouth (Isaiah 53:7).

He will suffer and die.

Truly our great Saviour trod the winepress of the cross alone. Not one of his disciples stood by him when he was arrested. He was a man of sorrows and suffering until his task was completed and he was able to rise up from the grave triumphant, having overcome Satan and his minions. He grasped the keys of death and hell and made an open show of the evil ones who had attempted to destroy him (Isaiah 52:13-53:12; 63:1-6; John 19:16-37; Ephesians 4: 7-10).

> *By oppression and judgement he was taken away. And who can speak of his descendants? For he was cut off from the land of the living; for the transgression of my people he was stricken* (Isaiah 53:8)

He will be assigned a grave with the wicked and the rich

When they knew Jesus, having been crucified between two thieves, was pronounced dead Joseph of Arimathea, a prince in Israel, asked for his body and then he buried him in his own tomb (John 19:38-42).

> *He was assigned a grave with the wicked, and with the rich in his death, though he had done no violence, neither was deceit in his mouth* (Isaiah 53:9).

He will rise again from the dead, overcoming death forever

By his resurrection Jesus overcame death forever and because of his victory we who have followed after him and accepted his salvation will also gain eternal life, the very life of God himself. We will be permitted to enter the garden and eat of the tree of life (Romans 1:1-4; Revelation 21:4; 22:1-6).

> *On this mountain he will destroy the shroud that enfolds all peoples, the sheet that covers all nations; he will swallow up death forever. The Sovereign Lord will wipe away the tears from all faces; he will remove the disgrace of his people from all the earth. The Lord has spoken* (Isaiah 25:7-8).

He will come a second time

Isaiah saw the Lord would come again in triumph to rule forever and he would come to reward those who had followed him (Revelation 1:4-8; Acts 1:9-11).

> *The Lord has made proclamation to the ends of the earth: Say to the Daughter of Zion, 'See, Your Saviour comes! See,*

his reward is with him, and his recompense accompanies him' (Isaiah 62:11; see also 59:20; Romans 11:26-27).

The day of the Messiah will come

There will come a day when the Lord will appear in the heavens and then men's hearts will fail and they will be filled with fear unless they have accepted Jesus as Saviour and been born again of the Spirit of God (2 Peter 3:1-13).

> *The Lord Almighty has a day in store for all the proud and lofty, for all that is exalted (and they will be humbled), ... Men will flee to the caves in the rocks and to holes in the ground from the dread of the Lord and the splendour of his majesty, when he rises to shake the earth* (Isaiah 2:12, 19; see also 13:6-13; 22:5).

The Messiah will sit on David's throne

> *Of the increase of his government and peace there will be no end. He will reign on David's throne and over his kingdom, establishing and upholding it with justice and righteousness from that time on forever. The zeal of the Lord Almighty will accomplish this* (Isaiah 9:7; see also 22:22).

The Messiah will be the judge

> *He will not judge by what he sees with his eyes, or decide by what he hears with his ears; but with righteousness he will judge the needy, with justice he will give decisions for the poor of the earth.. He will strike the earth with the rod of his mouth; with the breath of his lips he will slay the wicked. Righteousness will be his belt and faithfulness the sash around his waist.* (Is 11:3b-5; see also 59:16-21; 63:1-6).

The Messiah will rule on the earth and there will be:

- A time of justice – (Isaiah 9:7; 11:2-5; 16:5; 32:1-2 & 16-18).
- A time of God's authority – (9:6-7; 11:2-4; 59:16).

- A time of splendour – (4:2; 24:23; 33:17; 40:5; 60:13, 19; 66:18).
- A time of peace – (2:3-4; 9:6-7; 11:6-9; 19:23-25; 32:16-17; 35:8-10; 65:25).
- A time of healing – (32:1-4, 17; 35:5-6; 42:7).
- A time of feasting – (25:6; 30:23-24; 55:1-2).
- All nations will prosper – (18:7; 60:5-6, 11; 61:6; 66:12).
- The Holy Spirit will be poured out – (11:2; 32:15; 44:3).[23]

There will be a new heaven and a new earth

The idea of a new heaven and a new earth is somewhat strange to us and hard to understand. How will it come about? When will it be? What needs to happen before that day when the earth will be renewed? It is God's glory that he can say these things and prophesy in advance what will happen in the fullness of time.

> *Behold I will create new heavens and a new earth. The former things will not be remembered, nor will they come to mind* (Isaiah 65:17)

Whatever God decrees will come to pass, the proof of this is abundant in scripture. All the prophecies in Isaiah about the Messiah's first coming and his ministry on earth, his death and resurrection have been fulfilled. The rest will follow in God's time (Isaiah 24:19-23; 42:9; 66:22).

So this wonderful book of Isaiah has been written for our understanding and delight. Proving for all time that our God knows the end from the beginning. In response our task is to believe and meditate on the wonders of his majesty and explicit foreknowledge.

---

[23] Taylor, C. V, From an unpublished work *The Vision of Isaiah* – Christology in Isaiah

Chapter Ten:

Bible Portraits

The Bible as a whole reveals Jesus as the Saviour of the whole world, but then each individual Old Testament book portrays Jesus in some separate facet of the splendour of his character and ministry. In this chapter and the next I have listed each book with its theme and then a verse from the New Testament proving that Jesus fulfilled that aspect richly in his life and ministry. There are other similar lists, for Christ is revealed in many ways throughout the Bible. A complete list, covering aspects of Jesus found in each book from Genesis to Revelation has been granted me to share in this book. I have included this wonderful collection, *Christ in all the Scriptures* in 'Addendum One' of this book.

In Genesis he is the Creator(Genesis 1:1). Jesus is the one who flung the stars into space and created 500,000,000 galaxies, most of which have only recently been discovered by the astronomers. He is the one who created this world of ours with its beauty and order. He is the one who created us also to love him and enjoy him forever.

He made us in his image so that we too can have creative gifts and abilities to make things both useful and beautiful, but we cannot create life, that is God's prerogative alone.

The book of Genesis is the beginning of all things and the book of Revelation is the completion of God's revelation to mankind. Therefore in Genesis we see the fall of mankind and in Revelation we see mankind restored once again to open fellowship with God.

In the very first words of Genesis the Bible denies all of the false philosophies that have ever been brought forward by those who do not believe in God.

'In the beginning *God*'...denies Atheism with its doctrine of *no* God.

'In the beginning God'...denies Polytheism with its doctrine of *many* gods.

'In the beginning *God created*'...denies Fatalism with its doctrine of *chance*.

'In the beginning *God created*'...denies Evolution with its doctrine of infinite *becoming*.

'God created *heaven and earth*'...denies Pantheism which makes God and the universe identical.

God created *heaven and earth*'...denies Materialism which asserts the eternity of matter.[24]

In the New Testament we are left in no doubt that it was Jesus who created this world of ours:

> *In the past God spoke to our forefathers through the prophets at many times and in various ways, but in these last days he has spoken to us by his Son, whom he appointed heir of all things, and through whom he made the universe* (Hebrews 1:1-2)

In Exodus he is the Passover Lamb (Exodus 12:1-11). Before the world began God carefully planned the Passover feast. The story of the paschal lamb was a pictorial drama of the future sacrifice that Jesus, the creator of all, would make for our salvation. Precise instructions were given to ensure the Israelites would never forget the night they were rescued from slavery, and from the death of their firstborn, by the blood of the lamb sprinkled on the lintel of their doorways. It was at this time that God laid down another link in the prophecies concerning his Son who was to come to die for us. Not a single bone of the lamb's body was to be broken and

---

[24] Baxter, J. Sidlow; *Explore the Book;* 'Volume One'; Published by Marshall Morgan and Scott; 1951. Pg. 34

when Jesus died on the cross his legs were not broken as were the legs of the two thieves who were crucified either side of him, thus fulfilling the prophecy given almost 1500 years before (John 19:33-34).

In the New Testament the Apostle Paul reminds us that Jesus is indeed our Passover Lamb:

> *Get rid of the old yeast that you may be a new batch without yeast – as you really are. For Christ, our Passover lamb has been sacrificed* (1 Corinthians 5:7).

In Leviticus he is the Sacrifice for sin (Leviticus 16:34). Once every year the high priest had to make atonement for his own sins and the sins of his family and then for the sins of all of the people. The instructions for the sprinkling of the blood of the sacrificed animals was complicated and had to be done carefully and reverently. If any mistake was made the consequences were severe. Aaron could not go into the Most Holy Place whenever he chose to under pain of death, he had to go in after following precise instructions from the Lord. How different it is for us who live in the age of grace. We can enter the holiest through the blood of Jesus who has opened the way for us, we should appreciate this wonderful privilege (Hebrews 9:22-28).

The writer to the Hebrews portrays Jesus as our great High Priest, the perfect sacrifice for all of our sin:

> *Such a high priest meets our need – one who is holy, blameless, pure, set apart from sinners, exalted above the heavens. Unlike the other high priests, he does not need to offer sacrifices day after day, first for his own sins, and then for the sins of the people. He sacrificed for their sins once for all when he offered himself. For the law appoints as high priests men who are weak; but the oath, which came after the law, appointed the Son, who has been made perfect forever* (Hebrews 7:26-28*).*

In Numbers he is the One lifted up in the wilderness (Numbers 21:4-8). The Israelites became impatient many times during their wilderness wanderings and this time they began to complain bitterly to Moses. *'Why have you brought us up out of Egypt to die in the desert? There is no bread! There is no water! And we detest this miserable food!'* At this God's anger was kindled against them and some venomous snakes began to bite the people and many perished. The people then repented and begged Moses to pray the Lord would deliver them from the snakes. God instructed Moses to make a bronze snake and to put it up on a pole. When this was done any who were bitten by a snake could look up to the bronze snake and live. This is a marvellous picture of the Saviour who was lifted up on a cross for us. If we look to him we gain eternal life.

The New Testament ratifies this as a type, a prophetic picture, of Jesus who died that we might live:

> *Just as Moses lifted up the snake in the desert, so the Son of Man must be lifted up, that everyone who believes in him may have eternal life* (John 3:14)

In Deuteronomy he is the True Prophet (Deuteronomy 18:18). At Horeb the people were afraid of the voice and the fire of God and begged Moses to speak to God for them. God understood their weakness, and in his mercy he promised Moses that he would send another prophet like him from among the people. One into whose mouth he would put words. One who would tell them everything God commanded him to say. This was a picture of Christ who was to come in the fullness of time. Jesus came to show us what God was really like, and to bring us the words of life. There is also a word of warning from God for us here, *'If anyone does not listen to my words that the prophet speaks in my name, I myself will call him to account'* (Deuteronomy 18:19).

When Jesus came the common people heard him gladly, they saw his miracles and they knew instinctively he was the one who was to come:

> *After the people saw the miraculous sign that Jesus did, they began to say, 'Surely this is the Prophet who is to come into the world'* (John 6:14).

In Joshua he is the Captain of our Salvation (Joshua 5:13-15). Near Jericho Joshua was visited by a man with a drawn sword in his hand. He identified himself as Commander of the army of the Lord and Joshua immediately fell to his knees in recognition. He said, *'What message does my Lord have for his servant?'* The commander of the Lord's army replied, *'Take off your sandals, for the place where you are standing is holy'* (14b). This was a manifestation of Christ in his pre-existence before he allowed himself to be born into this world for our salvation. Now after his sacrificial death and triumphant resurrection are accomplished he is more than ever the Captain of our salvation.

Jesus suffered temptation as we do and though he remained without sin he was made perfect through suffering which culminated in his death on the cross. Therefore he understands our weaknesses and as the Captain of our salvation he leads and guides us, bringing us finally to safety.

> *For it became him, for whom are all things, and by whom are all things, in bringing many sons unto glory, to make* **the captain of their salvation** *perfect through sufferings. For both he that sanctifieth and they who are sanctified are all of one: for which cause he is not ashamed to call them brethren* (Hebrews 2:10-11 KJV)

In Judges he is the Deliverer Judge (Judges 3:9-11). In these verses Othniel is shown as a type of Christ the deliverer. During the time of the judges we are told there was no king so every man did as he saw fit (Judges 17:6). Time after time a new generation of the Israelites would grow up not having seen God's deliverance or the mighty miracles he wrought for their ancestors, because of this they frequently forgot God and slipped into idolatry. Each time this happened they would be overcome by an enemy and then they would cry out to God for deliverance. When they did this in repentant faith God would send them yet another deliverer. Othniel was one of these. He was the son of Caleb's younger brother Kenaz and in Judges chapter one we are told he won the hand of Caleb's daughter Acsah by attacking and capturing Kiriath Sepher. He was trained and successful in the art of war and fitted to be one of Israel's judges. The land had peace under his rule for forty years after he had overpowered Cushan-Rishathaim, king of Aram.

In the New Testament Jesus is the Judge who will come to judge the world when the time is right:

> *There is only one Lawgiver and Judge, the one who is able to save and destroy* (James 4:12a).

In Ruth he is the Kinsman Redeemer (Ruth 4:1-12). In this tender and touching story of the love of a daughter-in-law for her mother-in-law and of the love which grew slowly between Ruth and Boaz we see a type of Christ's love for the church and his power to redeem it. Ruth asked Boaz to be her protector and he arranged to redeem her The fruit of the union between Ruth and Boaz was their son Obed, who became the father of Jesse, who in turn was the father of David the warrior king and sweet singer of Israel. So we see God allowing a Moabitess to become part of the line from which our Saviour would be born into this world, thus including a Gentile in his plan of salvation.

In Christ we are redeemed from the kingdom of darkness and brought into his marvellous kingdom of light. Jesus is our Kinsman Redeemer, the one who has redeemed us by his precious blood and given us power to become sons and daughters of God (John 1:12).

> *In love he predestined us to be adopted as his sons through Jesus Christ, in accordance with his pleasure and will – to the praise of his glorious grace, which he has freely given us in the One he loves. In him we have redemption through his blood, the forgiveness of sins, in accordance with the riches of God's grace that he lavished on us with all wisdom and understanding* (Ephesians 1:5-8).

In 1 & 2 Samuel; 1 & 2 Kings; 1 & 2 Chronicles he is the King. David typifies the warrior king who overcomes the enemy and Solomon is a type of the wise and good king who brings peace and plenty to the land and its people. There are many fascinating stories of Israel's kings. Saul was chosen as the first king and when he failed David was anointed and became king after him. Later under the leadership of David's son Solomon Israel reached the pinnacle of its strength and riches as a nation. After that the decline set in and eventually because of the kingdom of Judah's continual rebellion and defiance of God they were taken into slavery for seventy years (Jeremiah 15:11-12; 29:10). Ezra and Nehemiah were anointed to return them to their native land where, in the fullness of time, the entrance of the Saviour into the world was accomplished. During all of their calamities the nation was finally delivered from its inclination to worship other gods and they remain true to their Lord today. In the great day of the Lord's coming they will look on Jesus whom they pierced and acknowledge him as their Messiah and Lord (Luke 13:35; Revelation 1:7).

In Revelation we are given the glorious picture of the King of Kings and Lord of Lords coming into his own at last, recognised as the Saviour and Lord of all:

> *I saw heaven standing open and there before me was a white horse, whose rider is called Faithful and True. With justice he judges and makes war. His eyes are like a blazing fire, and on his head are many crowns. He has a name written on him that no one knows but he himself. He is dressed in a robe dipped in blood, and his name is the Word of God. The armies of heaven were following him, riding on white horses and dressed in fine linen, white and clean. Out of his mouth comes a sharp sword with which to strike down the nations. He will rule them with an iron sceptre. He treads the winepress of the fury of the wrath of God Almighty. On his robe and on his thigh he has this name written: KING OF KINGS AND LORD OF LORDS (Re 19:11-16).*

In Ezra and Nehemiah he is the Restorer (Ezra 6:14). Ezra and Nehemiah restored three things, the walls of Jerusalem, the temple, and the reading of the word of God to the people. As Ezra restored the temple under the preaching of Haggai and Zechariah, he also restored the people's knowledge of God's word (Nehemiah 8:8). He read the law to the people and, with the help of the priests, made it clear to them so they could understand it. Because of this the nation repented of their sins and went through a period of restoration. The nation was restored and rebuilt under both Ezra and Nehemiah. These two were very different men with widely disparate gifts but both were greatly used of God for the restoration of Jerusalem and the rebuilding of the temple. Together they show Christ the ultimate restorer of all things.

Although much time has passed since the death and resurrection of Jesus we know God has promised that ultimately Christ will restore all things. Nothing can prevent God's plan from being fulfilled:

> *Repent, then, and turn to God, so that your sins may be wiped out, that times of refreshing may come from the Lord, and that he may send the Christ, who has been appointed for you – even Jesus. He must remain in heaven until the time comes for God to restore everything, as he promised long ago through his holy prophets* (Acts 3:19-21).

In Esther he is the Advocate (Esther 4:12-14). In this moving and thrilling story of a woman's faith and trust in the uncle who had reared her, and in the God she had been taught to obey implicitly, we see Christ as the advocate, the one who through his intercession helps us in our weakness. Esther risked her life to intercede for her people, not foolishly or without thoughtful preparation, but with much prayer and fasting and strong courage, based on her belief that God was in charge and that he would deliver her people from cruel Haman by a miracle of divine grace and mercy (7:1-6a). Haman in his implacable hatred of the Jews, typifies Satan in his desire to eliminate these precious people who were chosen by God as the vehicle to bring his Son into the world.

Jesus our compassionate High Priest is interceding for us constantly before the Father. He understands our weaknesses as he himself knew the force of temptation, though he did not give in to Satan's wiles, but kept himself pure in every way.

> *My dear children, I write this to you so that you will not sin. But if anybody does sin, we have one who speaks to the Father in our defense – Jesus Christ the Righteous One. He is the atoning sacrifice for our sins, and not only for ours but also for the sins of the whole world* (1 Jn 2:1-2).

In Job he is the Redeemer and Mediator (Job 19:25). Some scholars believe the book of Job is the oldest book in the Bible, perhaps written by Moses during his time in the desert. No one knows for sure, but it is an ancient book. It is therefore surprising that way back then in the mists of time Job knew so thoroughly that his Redeemer lived and that one day he would stand on the earth. This is one more definite and sure sign that the hand of God has been in the writing of the Bible since the very beginning (Hebrews 1:1).

In the book of Job we see Christ the Redeemer. Job was a real person though his story is told in the form of a dramatic poem for he was mentioned by the prophet Ezekiel who identifies Noah, Daniel and Job as servants of God (Ezekiel 14:14, 20). James also refers to the patience of Job (James 5:11).

Martin Luther regarded the book of Job as *'more magnificent and sublime than any other book of scripture.'* Though not a prophet Job gave witness to the Messiah, the one who was to come, predicting that he would be a Redeemer. Job knew that one day he would see his Redeemer (Job 19:25-27). Jesus himself said, *'I am alive for ever and ever'* (Revelation 1;17).

In Chapters 9-16 of the book of Job we see Job's intense desire for someone to stand in the gap. Bildad's first speech blames Job, insisting that Job's sufferings were caused by sin in his life! Job's reply insisted he was not wicked (Job 10:7) chastisement, he maintains, overtakes the righteous as well as the sinner. He then pleads for one able to judge between them.

> *If only there were someone to arbitrate between us, to lay his hand upon us both, someone to remove God's rod from me, so that his terror would frighten me no more. Then I would speak up without fear of him, but as it now stands with me, I cannot'* (Job 9:33-35).

Later when Job is accused by Eliphaz of stretching out his hand against God in Job chapter 15 he cries out in answer–

> *'Even now my witness is in heaven; my advocate is on high. My intercessor is my friend as my eyes pour out tears to God; on behalf of a man he pleads with God as a man pleads for his friend* (Job 16:19-21).

The patriarch Job finally found a partial mediator in Elihu, but our perfect mediator is Jesus our Lord who can take our part and God's part and bring us together in him!

An arbitrator must not only be just but he must have a clear understanding of the claims, complaints and character of each of the parties. Jesus is the perfect mediator as he is both God and man. At Calvary he reached out one hand to God and the other to sinful man (1 Timothy 2:5).

W.E.Vine comments on this:

> The salvation of men necessitated that the Mediator should himself have the nature and attributes of him toward whom he acts, and should likewise participate in the nature of those for whom he acts (sin apart); only by being possessed both of Deity and humanity could he comprehend the claims of the one and the needs of the other.[25]

---

[25] Vine, W. E. *Expository Dictionary of New Testament Words*; Mac Donald Publishing Co. Virginia; Reference: 'Mediator'; Pg. 736.

There is one who is our go-between, one who stands between us and God, that one is Jesus. He intercedes for us before the Father in heaven continually (Hebrews 9:15; 12:24).

> *For you know that it was not with perishable things such as silver or gold that you were redeemed from the empty way of life handed down to you from your forefathers, but with the precious blood of Christ, a lamb without blemish or defect* (1 Peter 1:18-19)

In Psalms he is the All in All (Psalm 24:8-10). He is the King of glory, now and forever, reigning in splendour in the heavens, and in our hearts also as we continue to do his will. He is likened to so many things in the book of Psalms, he is our rock, (Psalm 18:31) and our fortress, representing strength and security (Psalm 46:7) His words are flawless, like silver refined in a furnace of clay; as we read the Word it reflects the face of God to us. (Psalm 12:6). He is the finest of the wheat; the bread of heaven, and honey in the rock, (Psalm 81:16). Honey is pure and sweet, it is good for you and it is good for your health, honey in the rock is purity and sweetness encased in security. He is also a lamp to our feet to make our way plain (Psalm 119:105). Truly he is all we need and his fellowship satisfies our soul. Jesus is our all in all, he has supplied our salvation. All we need to do is accept that salvation and rest in it, as we are told in Hebrews –

> *In these last days he has spoken to us by his Son, whom he appointed heir of all things and through whom he made the universe. The Son is the radiance of God's glory and the exact representation of his being, sustaining all things by his powerful word. After he had provided purification for sins, he sat down at the right hand of the Majesty in heaven* (Hebrews 1:2-3).

In Proverbs he is Wisdom (Proverbs 8:1-21). The description of wisdom in Proverbs points to the character of Christ who was filled with all wisdom and knowledge. Wisdom has prudence and understanding; it speaks only truth, it is just; it has knowledge and discretion; it has counsel and sound judgment; it has power. The fruits of wisdom are riches and honour, wealth and prosperity, its fruit is better than fine gold and its yield surpasses silver. Wisdom walks in the way of righteousness, and along the paths of justice. We see wisdom was with God from the beginning, appointed from eternity before the world began. Jesus is typified here as wisdom, working alongside God in the creation of the world.

Jesus has this kind of wisdom and he showed it many times during his earthly walk among men.

> *And Jesus grew in wisdom and stature, and in favour with God and man* (Lu 2:52).

Chapter Eleven:

More Bible Portraits

In Ecclesiastes he is the Judge of all (Ecclesiastes 12:13-14). The wise king Solomon with all his riches learned all he could, studied the wonders of this world of ours, and then came to the conclusion that the whole duty of man is to fear God and keep his commands. This is the way to contentment, for if we live our life in this way we will escape his judgment. When the time comes he will examine all our deeds and every hidden thing that is in our heart. Those of us who are in Christ have the task of examining ourselves during the communion service and allowing the word of God to judge us now so that when that time comes we will be safe from judgment (1 Corinthians 11:23-32).

One day time will be no more, Jesus will come as judge of this whole world and everyone who has ever lived will stand before him.

> *Then I saw a great white throne and him who was seated on it. Earth and sky fled from his presence, and there was no place for them. And I saw the dead great and small, standing before the throne, and books were opened. Another book was opened, which is the book of life. The dead were judged according to what they had done as recorded in the books* (Re 20:11-12).

In the Song of Solomon he is the Lover of our Souls (Song of Songs 1:1-4). His name is as perfume poured into our lives. He is our bridegroom as well as our Saviour and he has proved this by redeeming us to God, and gaining for us freedom from the power of sin and by leading us into sweet fellowship with himself. We prove our love for him by obeying his commands and he proves his for us by revealing himself to us in all his glory and sweetness. Comparing Psalm 45 with the Song of Solomon gives us even more idea of the beauty of our King of kings and how he longs to purify and adorn his bride, the church, and prepare her for his coming.

In John's gospel Jesus tells us how we can prove our love for him, by our obedience to his commands.

> *Whoever has my commands and obeys them, he is the one who loves me. He who loves me will be loved by my Father, and I too will love him and show myself to him* (Jn 14:21).

In Isaiah he is the Messiah (Isaiah 53:1-12). Isaiah more than any other Old Testament writer has revealed our Saviour in all his wonder as our Messiah, the anointed one of God. Isaiah reveals to us in his verses the result of the suffering of Christ our Saviour. He who has borne our sin and rescued us from eternal death will be satisfied with the results when he makes up his treasured possession (Malachi 3:16-18). He is now highly exalted above every name that is named and eventually every knee will bow to him and acknowledge him as Lord (Colossians 1:15-17).

Jesus knew who he was and what his future task was and he was bold to announce his coming ministry before his family and friends.

> *The scroll of the prophet Isaiah was handed to him (Jesus). Unrolling it, he found the place where it is written: 'The Spirit of the Lord is upon me because he has anointed me to preach good news to the poor. He has sent me to proclaim freedom for the prisoners and recovery of sight for the blind, to release the oppressed, to proclaim the year of the Lord's favour'* (Lu 4:17-19).

In Jeremiah and Lamentations he is the Righteous Branch (Jeremiah 31:31-34). In Jeremiah we are promised the righteousness which comes to us freely from God because of our Saviour's efforts on our behalf. There is no way we can earn our own righteousness, it has to come to us from Jesus. His law has to be put into our minds and written on our hearts by the Lord, without this we can never please our God in any way. Our salvation comes from Jesus and from Jesus alone. If we try to gain our own salvation, or to do something toward it, this stems from pride. No, we must give up our own efforts and gladly accept the salvation given to us through Jesus our Righteous Branch.

The writer to the Hebrews gives us a revelation of the present exalted heavenly position of Jesus our Saviour.

> *But about the Son he says, Your throne, O God, will last for ever and ever, and righteousness will be the sceptre of your kingdom. You have loved righteousness and hated wickedness: therefore God, your God, has set you above your companions by anointing you with the oil of joy* (He 1:8-9).

In Ezekiel he is the Son of Man (Ezekiel 2:1-9). Ezekiel was sent by God to speak to a rebellious, obstinate and stubborn people, the people of Israel. Jesus came to the same people and they were still just as stubborn and stiff necked as ever. Those in authority would not listen to Jesus but hated him and eventually killed him. Jesus often referred to himself as the Son of Man. The common people, those who were unable to keep all of the extra laws laid upon them by the Pharisees and teachers of the law, heard him gladly. Jesus set them free from the guilt they had been feeling, that was put upon them by the Pharisees who, Jesus said, '*strained out gnats and swallowed camels!*' They kept the letter of the law but neglected the more important matters of that same law, justice, mercy and faithfulness (Matthew 23:23-24).

Jesus was truly God but also truly man. In his humanity as Son of Man he suffered as we do with weariness, hunger and loneliness; he had no permanent home.

> *Jesus replied, 'Foxes have holes and birds of the air have nests, but the Son of Man has no place to lay his head* (Mt 8:20 *see also* Mk 2:3-12).

In Daniel he is the Smiting Stone (Daniel 2:44-45). In Daniel's vision, given to him so that he could explain the dream of king Nebuchadnezzar, the rock that struck the statue of gold and bronze, iron and clay, became a huge mountain and filled all the earth. This was a vision of the Saviour Jesus, the smiting stone, and the kingdom of God to come that would eliminate all other kingdoms. God will set up a kingdom which will never be destroyed. When he heard these things explained to him, king Nebuchadnezzar fell prostrate before Daniel and paid him honour and ordered that an offering and incense be presented to him. Then the king said to Daniel, *'Surely your God is the God of gods and the Lord of kings and a revealer of mysteries, for you were able to reveal this mystery'* (Daniel 2:47).

In the New Testament Jesus is referred to as the corner stone or capstone. He is our perfect example and we must walk in his steps. To those who do not accept him he will be a rock of offense.

> *Now to you who believe, this stone is precious, But to those who do not believe, The stone the builders rejected has become the capstone and, a stone that causes men to stumble and a rock that makes them fall* (1 Pe 2:7-8).

In Hosea he is the Healer of the backslider (Hosea 3:1-5). This story of the incredible love of Hosea for his erring wife and the gentle way he restored her to his home typifies the Lord who loved Israel despite her many shortcomings and her lusting after other gods. He knew he would win his people to himself eventually so he gave instructions to Hosea to reclaim his wife. This merciful act gave Israel a picture of God's everlasting love for them. By the time God gave the people of the kingdom of Judah the opportunity to return to their native land, after the seventy years of captivity prophesied by Jeremiah were completed, they were thoroughly his. They knew they had missed their opportunity to be a great nation and take their message to the world but they were determined now to live right and keep God's laws. They had synagogues set up throughout the land where people could go and hear the word of

God read and explained to them. The scene was set for the coming of the Messiah.

In the New Testament Jesus shows himself the healer of the backslider. He was gentle with Peter who denied him three times and asked him three times, *'Do you love me?'* Finally Peter broke down and said, *'You know all things, you know I love you.'* He was healed from that hour of his shame and humiliation caused by his three denials, and went on to do great exploits for God. (John 21:15-19).

Jesus restores those who falter and fail as he shows so well in his parable of the prodigal son.

> *So he (the prodigal son) got up and went to his father. But while he was still a long way off, his father saw him and was filled with compassion for him; he ran to his son, threw his arms around him and kissed him* (Luke 15:20).

In Joel he is the Restorer (Joel 2:25-29). In Joel we are promised that our past sins will be forgiven and somehow, in his sovereignty, God will eliminate our past sin when in sorrowful repentance we reach out in faith to believe in Jesus. He will recycle our disreputable and sinful past and redeem our dross to usefulness. His righteousness will cover all our sin and make us fit for his service. Then he will fill us with his Holy Spirit and glory in using us to further his kingdom. In every way Jesus is the restorer of our past and the architect of our future as we make ourselves available to him.

It is through the baptism in the Holy Spirit that we gain revelation of who we are in Christ and the understanding of our future inheritance.

> *And you also were included in Christ when you heard the word of truth, the gospel of your salvation. Having believed, you were marked in him with a seal, the promised Holy Spirit, who is a deposit guaranteeing our inheritance until*

the redemption of those who are God's possession - to the praise of his glory (Ephesians 1:13-14).

In Amos he is the Heavenly Husbandman (Amos 9:11-15). Here is a promise not only to restore the ruins and rebuild the broken places but also to sow and reap abundantly. The picture is of plenty, of more than plenty, of super abundance. Crops will grow and develop so rapidly that the reaper will overtake the sower and spring and summer will combine to bring an overflowing richness to the land. The promise is to broken lives, that they will be healed and rebuilt to the glory of God, Not only refashioned to usefulness but full to overflowing with happiness and joy they will not be able to contain. Blessing will flow out from them to others as they yield their lives to Jesus who is the heavenly husbandman, the one who can make all things new.

Jesus assures us in the gospel of John that he is the vine and we are the branches, it is through him we bear fruit. He also warns us that we must remain in him.

> *I am the true vine, and my Father is the gardener. He cuts off every branch in me that bears no fruit, while every branch that does bear fruit he prunes so that it will be even more fruitful (John 15:1-2).*

In Obadiah he is the Saviour (Obadiah 1:21). The kingdom will be the Lord's kingdom and he is the deliverer. Our very present help in time of trouble. No one delivers like our Jesus; no one can stand before him. He is our Saviour, he has earned the title of deliverer for he trod the winepress alone and made a way for us to be redeemed.

In Paul's instructions to Titus he portrays Jesus as our great God, our redeemer from all evil who will perfect us and prepare us for his service.

> *...while we wait for the blessed hope – the glorious appearing of our great God and Saviour, Jesus Christ, who gave himself for us to redeem us from all wickedness and to purify*

for himself a people that are his very own, eager to do what is good (Titus 2:13-14).

In Jonah he is the Resurrection and Life (Jonah 2:7-9). As Jonah was in the belly of the great fish for three days and nights and then was delivered by being vomited out on to dry land, he was a type of Jesus spending three days in the tomb and then being raised from the dead to prove he is the Son of God (Romans 1:1-4).

Jesus is the resurrection and the life to each believer who trusts in him.

I am the resurrection and the life. He who believes in me will live, even though he dies; and whoever lives and believes in me will never die (John 11:25).

In Micah he is a Witness against rebellious nations (Micah 4:1-5). One day Jesus will reign and of his kingdom there will be no end. There will be no more war, peace will reign and all will be well. Nations will seek to know him and to walk in his ways.

When the Son of Man comes in his glory, and all the angels with him, he will sit on his throne in heavenly glory. All the nations will be gathered before him, and he will separate the people one from another as a shepherd separates the sheep from the goats (Matthew 25:31-32).

In Nahum he is a Stronghold in the day of trouble (Nahum 1:7). Jesus is a stronghold, a fortress where we can hide from trouble. All who love him and fear him will be safe in that great day when the books of God are opened and the dead are judged.

Peace I leave with you; my peace I give you. I do not give to you as the world gives. Do not let your hearts be troubled and do not be afraid (John 14:27). *I have told you these things, so that in me you may have peace. In this world you will have trouble. But take heart I have overcome the world* (16:33).

In Habakkuk he is the God of our Salvation (Habakkuk 3:17-19). Here the prophet Habakkuk affirms that no matter what calamities may overtake him he will not be moved away from his faith in God. In the same way we who belong to Jesus believe that he is with us at all times, no matter what disaster overtakes us in this life he will never leave us or forsake us (Hebrews 13:5b-6). He is our salvation, he is our freedom; Jesus is with us always, even to the end of the age.

> *In this (salvation) you greatly rejoice , though for a little while you may have had to suffer grief in all kinds of trials. These have come so that your faith – of greater worth than gold, which perishes even though refined by fire– may be proved genuine and may result in praise, glory and honour when Jesus Christ is revealed* (1 Peter 1:6-7).

In Zephaniah he is a Loving Father (Zephaniah 3:17). Here is a tender picture of God's love; it is of a father singing his little one to sleep as he rejoices over him. Jesus the Son of God is also the loving Father, we are told in Isaiah that one of his names would be everlasting Father (Isaiah 9:6b). Here he shows the great love he bears us, he quiets us with his love, and he rejoices over us with singing. How could we ever doubt the love he bears us or turn away from that love?

We should remind ourselves of these verses when the enemy of our souls tries to tell us we are unloved and that we are useless to the King. Do not listen to Satan for he is the father of lies, lying is his native language! (John 8:44).

> *Anyone who has seen me has seen the Father* (John 14:9).

In Haggai he is the Desire of all nations (Haggai 2:7). God has promised that one day the desire of all nations will come. That is Jesus our Saviour, for he is the desire of all nations, even though they do not realise this truth as yet. He will come and reign forever on the throne of his kingdom. Then there will be peace at last for all his enemies will be vanquished.

Jesus will judge between the nations, the sheep and the goats (Matthew 25:31-46)

> *After this I looked and there before me was a great multitude that no one could count, from every nation, tribe, people, and language, standing before the throne and in front of the Lamb. They were wearing white robes and were holding palm branches in their hands. And they cried out in a loud voice. 'Salvation belongs to our God, who sits on the throne, and to the Lamb'* (Revelation 7:9-10).

In Zechariah he is the Righteous King (Zechariah 9:9). This verse is a prophecy of the time of Jesus triumphant entry into Jerusalem. All those years before God knew and had planned that Jesus would ride into Jerusalem on a donkey, and the prophecy was so accurate that it described the animal as a colt, the foal of a donkey. And this was fulfilled in all its detail (Luke 19:28-38).

God knows the end from the beginning and sees the future that he has decreed as if it had already come to pass. Jesus came to Jerusalem as their righteous king and many greeted him gladly but the rulers hated him and encompassed his death on the cross. This too was God's plan and it was for the salvation of all that Jesus was willing to die. Now he is our righteous king and he will reign forever. Jesus planned ahead for his triumphant entry into Jerusalem. As the donkey was unbroken Jesus was able to show his perfect control over his creation by riding it without any trouble, even in that crowd of shouting, praising people waving palm branches.

> *When he came near the place where the road goes down to the Mount of Olives, the whole crowd of disciples began joyfully to praise God in loud voices for all the miracles they had seen: 'Blessed is the king who comes in the name of the lord. Peace in heaven and glory in the highest'* (Luke 19:37-38).

In Malachi he is the Son of Righteousness (Malachi 4:2). Here is a marvellous picture of our Saviour as a brilliant sun arising into a new dawn bringing healing in its rays as they pour down upon the earth. He is truly the Son of righteousness who has healing in his wings. He is the Son of God who has strength and power and glory to save and heal and sweep many souls into his kingdom.

> *People brought all their sick to him and begged him to let the sick just touch the edge of his cloak, and all who touched him were healed* (Matthew 14:35b-36).

Chapter Twelve:

The Claims of Jesus

What did Jesus claim for himself? What did others claim for him? So far we have examined many of the overwhelming proofs of Jesus claim to be the Son of the living God. In this chapter and the next we will catch a brief glimpse into his life and ministry, what he claimed for himself, the testimony of others as to his Messianic call, and a final meditation on our Lord and Saviour.

He Laid Aside His Godhead

Before entering this world of ours in the form of a helpless infant Jesus had to lay aside his infinite powers. He knew that when the time came for him to begin his ministry he would have to confine himself to the acts of a man empowered by the Holy Spirit. Therefore Jesus did not perform any miracles that had not already been foreshadowed by the prophets. They were ordinary men, yet because of their earnest prayers and the anointing of the Holy Spirit, they were able to manipulate the elements, (earth, air, fire and water) to multiply food, and to heal the sick and raise the dead.

Moses parted the Red Sea (Exodus 14:15-21) and twice brought forth water from a rock, (Exodus 17:5-7; Numbers 20:6-13). Elijah prayed for drought and had his prayer answered, (1 Kings 17:1) then prayed for rain and the drought was broken (1 Kings 18:41-45). He called down fire from heaven, (1 Kings 18:36-38; 2Kings 1:1-12) multiplied the meal and oil of the widow of Zarephath, (1 Kings 17:7-16) went over Jordan dry shod, (2 Kings 2:7-8) and raised one boy to life (1 Kings 17:17-24). Elisha, among many similar miracles, also went over Jordan dry shod, (2 Kings 2:11-14) multiplied bread to feed a hundred men, (2 Kings 4:42-44) healed Naaman the leper, (2 Kings 5:1-19) and raised a dead boy to life again (2 Kings 4:8-36).

Jesus also manipulated the elements, by turning water into wine during the wedding at Cana, (John 2:1-11) and by calming the storm on the sea of Galilee (Matthew 8:23-27). He also multiplied food, (Matthew 14:13-21) healed the sick, (Matthew 9:35-38) and raised the dead (Luke 7:11-17; Luke 8:49-56; John 11:38-44) but he moved in even more power and performed a greater number of miracles than the prophets as he had the Holy Spirit without any limit (John 3:34)

During his forty day fast following his baptism in the Jordan, Jesus was tempted of the devil in three different areas and he answered each time with the word of God. *'It is written'* (Luke 4:1-13). These temptations were a blatant attempt by the devil to get Jesus to resume his heavenly powers.

Had he turned the stones into bread during his temptation in the wilderness then that would have been taking back his Godhead, and reclaiming the powers he had put aside when he had agreed to enter our world in human form. He could not do this without aborting his whole mission.

The Challenge of Jesus

This challenge was given by Jesus to the Jews who sought to kill him because he called God his Father, thus making himself equal with God.

> *I have testimony weightier than that of John. For the very work that the Father has given me to finish, and which I am doing, testifies that the Father has sent me. And the Father who sent me has himself testified concerning me. You have never heard his voice nor seen his form, nor does his word dwell in you, for you do not believe the one he sent. You diligently study the scriptures because you think that by them you possess eternal life. These are the scriptures that testify about me, yet you refuse to come to me to have life* (John 5:36-40).

The Authority of Jesus

The authority with which Jesus spoke astounded the Jews. They had never heard anyone speak with such authority before. Always when the Rabbis spoke they supported their arguments by quoting from others, much as we do when preaching today. The prophets too always said, *'Thus says the Lord,'* as their authority was a delegated authority coming from God. Jesus, on the other hand spoke with authority because he had been given that authority by God, he was authority itself, and he had no need to appeal to anyone else to back his words.

> *When Jesus had finished saying these things, the crowds were amazed at his teaching, because he taught as one who had authority, and not as their teachers of the law* (Matthew 7:28-29).

At the very beginning of his ministry he stood up in the synagogue and read from Isaiah:

> *The Spirit of the Lord is on me, because he has anointed me to preach good news to the poor. He has sent me to proclaim freedom for the prisoners and recovery of sight for the blind, to release the oppressed, to proclaim the year of the Lord's favour* (Isaiah 61:1-3; Luke 4:18-19).

At first all of the people spoke well of him and were amazed at the gracious words that came from his lips (Luke 4:22) but then when he went on to indicate that the Gentiles were as important as the Jews, if not more beloved by God than they were, because he had cared for the widow of Zarephath, and cleansed Naaman the leper, and he had not done these things for any of his chosen people at that time (4:24-27). These words made the people, many of whom must have been his close relatives, to feel a murderous rage against Jesus. They attempted to kill him, but he walked right through the crowd and went on his way serene in the knowledge that no one could harm him until the time came for him to be arrested and crucified.

The Testimony of Jesus

Jesus, during the three and a half years of his ministry, had supreme confidence in God his Father, he knew who he was and why he had been born into this world. Many times he claimed his uniqueness –.

> *All things have been committed to me by my Father. No one knows who the Son is except the Father, and no one knows who the Father is except the Son and those to whom the Son chooses to reveal him* (Luke 10:22).
>
> *Then Jesus declared, 'I am the bread of life. He who comes to me will never go hungry, and he who believes in me will never be thirsty'* (John 6:35)
>
> *I am the gate; whoever enters through me will be saved. He will come in and go out and find pasture* (John 10:9).
>
> *When Jesus spoke again to the people, he said, 'I am the light of the world. Whoever follows me will never walk in darkness, but will have the light of life* (John 8:12).
>
> *Jesus said to her, 'I am the resurrection and the life. He who believes in me will live, even though he dies, and whoever lives and believes in me will never die* (John 11:25-26a)
>
> *Jesus answered, 'I am the way the truth and the life. No one comes to the Father except through me* (John 14:6).
>
> *Philip said, 'Lord show us the Father, and that will be enough for us.' Jesus answered, 'Don't you know me, Philip, even after I have been among you such a long time. Anyone who has seen me has seen the Father, How can you say, 'Show us the Father'? Don't you believe that I am in the Father, and that the Father is in me? The words I say to you are not just my own. Rather it is the Father living in me, who is doing his work* (John 14:8-10).

The Healing Ministry of Jesus

The healings that were performed by Jesus throughout his ministry were proof that he was the Son of God sent into the world to proclaim the kingdom of God. He fulfilled the prophecies concerning the ministry of the Messiah who was to come by preaching the good news to the poor, healing the sick, binding up the broken hearted, setting free the captives, and comforting the mourners (Isaiah 61:1-3).

Everyone who came to him with faith in their heart received their healing, no one was turned aside. In this way he fulfilled the prophecies concerning himself as a deliverer (Isaiah 35:5-6). He had compassion on his people who were like sheep without a shepherd, wandering in a world of sin and sickness and diseases of all kinds and he healed all who came to him believing. (Matthew 9:35-38).

He proved he had power over Satan by setting people free from satanic bondages (Matthew 8:28-34; 17:14-18; Mark 1:21-28; 32-34; 9:14-27).

Jesus, who had perfect discernment of the hearts of men and women (John 2:24), healed only those who came to him with faith to be healed. (Matthew 9:27-30). It is interesting to note that after Jesus returned to his Father there were still many sick people in Israel. Think about the people around the pool of Bethesda where Jesus healed only one person, and even more interestingly, the cripple at the Beautiful gate of the temple, for Jesus must have passed him many times during his ministry. Obviously there were many others also that Jesus bypassed because of the number of people who were still sick after Pentecost (Acts 5:16).

He Chose His Disciples Well

In choosing the twelve from among his disciples Jesus showed great wisdom. He picked twelve men from the upper middle class who were able to spend the time to be taught by him over a period of three years. He asked three sets of brothers to follow him.

Andrew and Peter, and James and John, two of the three, were partners in the fishing business and so knew and trusted each other (Luke 5:8-10). It is possible also that James and John were cousins of Jesus, as their mother Salome may have been sister to Mary, the mother of Jesus.

> Although it is not certain Salome and Mary were sisters, if it were so it would make James and John cousins of Jesus. This would help explain Salome's request of Jesus on behalf of her sons (Matthew 20:20-28).[26]

Certainly James the less and Thaddeus, the third set of brothers, were cousins of Jesus, as their father Cleopas (Alpheus) was brother to Joseph the husband of Mary, as we established in chapter one of this book. When you remember also that Elizabeth, the mother of John the Baptist was a relative of Mary (Luke 1:36), then you begin to see what a blessed and chosen family this was.[27]

The others chosen by Jesus were not related, but they too were also upper middle class men, Matthew (Levi) was a tax collector, and as such was looked upon as a collaborator with the Romans; Simon the Zealot was one of a small number of Jews known for their zeal in religion. The Zealots were fanatical nationalists who were striving to bring the coming of the Messiah closer to fruition by their efforts. The fact that these two, Matthew and Simon, could live in close fellowship with one another for three years shows the strength of the love and tolerance Jesus was able to nurture in his disciples. Philip was a native of Bethsaida, the city of Andrew and Peter; Nathanael (Bartholomew) was brought to Jesus by Philip, (John 1:44-45) and these two were friends who probably went out together when Jesus sent out the twelve to evangelise, (Luke 9:1-2). Then there were Thomas (Didymus) the twin, and Judas who became the traitor.

---

[26] *Op cit. John the Apostle;* Art.

[27] *Ibid.*

This close knit team of men were prayerfully called and trained by Jesus and, apart from Judas, they all served well in their future ministry.

The Testimony of The Disciples

Peter, who was not always wise in speech, nevertheless was the first one to receive revelation and to proclaim Jesus as the Messiah of Israel (Mark 8:27-30). Later, after he had gone through great agony of soul, because of denying Christ three times on the night he was arrested, Peter finally came to the end of himself and his own weakness and cowardice. After he was anointed at Pentecost, Peter became a leader of the disciples and was greatly used by God. So much so that people strove to have even his shadow pass over them, believing it was enough to bring healing to their bodies. (Acts 5:12-16).

Thomas, originally a doubter of the resurrection of Jesus, had those doubts completely overcome by seeing and feeling the wounds of Jesus' crucifixion (John 20:24-29).

Acts tells us that after his suffering, and across a period of forty days, Jesus gave his disciples many convincing proofs of his resurrection, and also spoke to them about the kingdom of God (Acts 1:3). All the disciples, apart from Judas, were witnesses of Jesus' solid resurrection body. They saw him eat some broiled fish, and they were shown his wounds (Luke 24:36-49). They spent time with him by the shores of Galilee, and he cooked them breakfast and talked with them about the future. It was here that Jesus reinstated Peter and gave him a new commission (John 21:1-25). Later, with about five hundred other believers, the disciples watched his ascension back into his Father's presence (Acts 1:9-11).

The Testimony of Paul

Paul was also an apostle, born abnormally because he was not called to be an apostle until after the day of Pentecost (1 Corinthians 15:8). He was especially chosen by Jesus to be an apostle to the Gentiles (Acts 9:15). He was a Hebrew of the Hebrews, a descendent of Abraham, of the tribe of Benjamin, a Pharisee and a member of the Sanhedrin (Philippians 3:4-6). Born in Tarsus Paul was also a Roman citizen.

Paul was a thoughtful scholar, a devout Jew, well trained under Gamaliel, a teacher of the law (Acts 22:3). Paul knew Jewish history and culture, he was familiar with Old Testament scripture, and well-read in the philosophies of Greece and Rome. He was finally conquered by a vision of the Saviour on the Damascus road (Acts 9:1-19), and he went on to become the greatest of the servants of Christ, spreading the gospel throughout the Gentile world.

Before his conversion he was so fanatical about the Jewish religion that he persecuted the infant church, imprisoning many and consenting to the murder of Stephen (Acts 8:1-3). Of all the people of Israel, he had most to lose by accepting Christ as his Saviour and Lord: but after his Damascus road experience his ringing testimony to the fact that Jesus is the Son of God was given first in Acts and then in his letters to the infant church –

> *Brothers, children of Abraham, and you God-fearing Gentiles, it is to us this message of salvation has been sent. The people of Jerusalem and their rulers did not recognise Jesus, <u>yet in condemning him they fulfilled the words of the prophets that are read every Sabbath</u>. We tell you the good news: What God promised our fathers he has fulfilled for us, their children, by raising up Jesus. As it is written in the second Psalm: '<u>You are my Son; today have I become your Father</u>'. The fact that God raised him from the dead, never to decay, is stated in these words: 'I will give you the holy and sure blessings promised to David'. So it is stated elsewhere: '<u>You will not let your Holy One see decay</u>' (Acts 13:26-27; 32-35).*

> *Paul, a servant of Christ Jesus, called to be an apostle and set apart for the gospel of God – the gospel he promised*

> *beforehand through his prophets in the Holy Scriptures regarding his Son, who as to his human nature was a descendent of David, and through the Spirit of holiness was declared with power to be the Son of God by his resurrection from the dead; Jesus Christ our Lord* (Romans 1:1-4).
>
> *Christ is the visible likeness of the invisible God. He is the first-born Son, superior to all created things. For through him God created everything in heaven and on earth, the seen and the unseen things, including spiritual powers, lords, rulers and authorities. God created the whole universe through him and for him. Christ existed before all things, and in union with him all things have their proper place* (Colossians 1:15-17 GNB).

Before his death by martyrdom under the Romans, Paul was able to establish and nurture many churches, and his letters to those various churches comprise a great part of the New Testament. It may be that without Paul's contribution the church would have remained a Jewish sect. However, in his foreknowledge, God called and equipped Paul to do the work of establishing the doctrines of the church. This cemented the foundations of the infant church and made it certain that it would not only survive but would literally *'turn the world upside down'*.

Chapter Thirteen:

Jesus The One and Only Son

God Knew From the Beginning

God the Father knew before the universe was established that we would have to be rescued from the hands of Satan and he determined to send Jesus, who was willing to become our Saviour, and so God's plan was laid out from the beginning.

What a marvellous Saviour we have, and how gracious he was to leave the comfort of heaven and to enfold himself into the confines of the flesh of a little babe. There Jesus patiently waited out the time needed for him to reach manhood before he could begin his journey to the cross.

Psalm 45 shows us a beautiful picture of Christ and his bride the church in type, and in it we catch a glimpse of what his life was like in the glory of heaven, and what he was prepared to leave for a season so that we might be delivered from evil.

> *Your throne, O God, will last forever and ever; a sceptre of justice will be the sceptre of your kingdom. You love righteousness and hate wickedness, therefore God, your God, has set you above your companions by anointing you with the oil of joy. All your robes are fragrant with myrrh and aloes and cassia; from palaces adorned with ivory the music on the strings makes you glad* (Psalm 45:6-8).

Who is this unique Jesus, prophesied from the very beginning to be our Saviour and our Deliverer from Satan's bondage? The ultimate answer is seen clearly in John's gospel: *The Word became flesh and made his dwelling among us. We have seen his glory, the glory of the One and Only who came from the Father, full of grace and truth* (John 1:14).

Here from the New Testament are five word pictures of Christ, the Messiah of Israel –

Jesus – Image of God and Artistic Creator

He is first of all the image of the invisible God. The Greek word for 'image' is '*eikon*', and Jesus in his incarnation came to represent God to us, he came to show us what God is like. Indeed, in the gospels he manifests God to us. In him we see God in action.

> *The Son is the radiance of God's glory and the exact representation of his being, sustaining all things by his powerful word* (Hebrews 1:3).

Jesus is the very image or impress of God's substance. Almost as a coin is impressed with the needed characters to make it legitimate coinage, so Jesus, made out of the very same substance as God the Father, was impressed with his image.

> *He is the image of the invisible God, the first born over all creation. For by him all things were created; things in heaven and on earth, visible and invisible, whether thrones or powers or rulers or authorities; all things were created by him and for him. He is before all things, and in him all things hold together* (Colossians 1:15-17).

This scripture in Colossians asserts Jesus true and absolute Godhead.

Henry Liddon had this to say about Jesus –

> He is both personally distinct from, and yet literally equal to him of whose essence he is the adequate imprint. [28]

What would God be doing if he were to appear here on earth today? He would do exactly what Jesus did. He would preach about the kingdom of heaven and he would heal the sick and he

---

[28] Liddon, H. P. (1829-1890) High Church of England divine; He wrote several volumes of sermons.

would teach. Whoever came to him would be accepted and loved. Those who opposed him would be rebuked. We know this because Jesus said to his disciple Phillip: *'Anyone who has seen me has seen the Father'* (Jn 14:9b).

And then second, he is our wonderful creator. We see his love of beauty and his artistry, in the world he made for us. The shapes, the unity and conformity within seeming chaos, leave us overwhelmed. He shows an infinite variety of expression in the multiplied colours of the exquisitely shaped flowers and the flocks of birds of every hue; and also in the seemingly infinite number of greens he has created in the leaves of the trees and shrubs which are so restful to our eyes.

The mighty mountains and the gleaming seas, the variety of creatures visible and invisible to the naked eye, all show his great genius. Indeed it is only in the last three hundred years, since the invention of the microscope, that we have been able to see his enormous capacity to create in microcosm as well as well as in macrocosm.

The stars in the night sky in all their twinkling beauty, show the Might and the Glory that belong to Jesus, the creator of each and every one– *The heavens declare the glory of God; the skies proclaim the work of his hands* (Psalm 19:1).

> *Lift up your eyes and look to the heavens; who created all these? He who brings out the starry host one by one, and calls them each by name. Because of his great power and mighty strength, not one of them is missing* (Isaiah 40:26).

In 1979 we took two of our sons to see the Parkes radio telescope. We were all impressed by the testimony of the Parkes' astronomers who said, 'We have to believe in God because we set our watches by the stars and they are always on time!'

Now with the Hubble telescope we are able to see photographs of the vast reaches of space and the seemingly infinite number of galaxies Jesus created.

How did Jesus create all this that we can see and know? How did he do it? He spoke and the work was done (Genesis 1:1). Because we are created in his image, in a sense we too can create by our words; we create blessing and healing if we speak positive words. In contrast, if we are not careful in our speech and we speak negatively, we can create unhappiness and sorrow. We need to be very careful in our speech (Matthew 12:34-37; James 3:9-10).

Jesus the Holy One

The Greek word for character *(charakter)* is almost equivalent in spelling to our English word. The terms 'character' and 'personality' are subtly different. Our character comprises our belief system, and our personality is the vehicle by which we present our character to the people around us. The character of Jesus during his time on earth was a holy character, and it is still a holy character.

From his birth he was holy. The angel Gabriel told Mary that because the Holy Spirit would overshadow her to create the babe in her womb, Jesus would be born holy. Gabriel assured Mary – *The Holy Spirit will come upon you and the power of the Most High will overshadow you. So the holy one to be born will be called the Son of God* (Luke 1:35).

Because he was born by the overshadowing of the Holy Spirit, Jesus was not contaminated as we are by the sin of disobedience perpetrated by Adam and Eve in the Garden of Eden, and he remained holy throughout his life by using the word of God against temptation (Luke 4).

The demons all knew Jesus was holy. They shouted out in their agony –

> *'What do you want with us, Jesus of Nazareth? Have you come to destroy us. I know who you are – the Holy One of God'* (Mark 1:24).

Jesus showed his holy character by his words and actions. He was courageous as well as holy, boldly proclaiming the word of truth. He was never worried or anxious, for he had perfect trust in his

Father. He loved to give freely, he related well to people, and he was full of love and compassion toward them.

Jesus the Compassionate Healer

Over and over in scripture we are told that, *'he healed them all'*. Imperfections could not exist in his presence, for he even touched the lepers and brought them healing; he had compassion on everyone.

> *Jesus went around visiting all the towns and villages. He taught in the synagogues, preached the Good News about the Kingdom and healed people with every kind of disease and sickness. As he saw the crowds, his heart was filled with pity for them, because they were worried and helpless, like sheep without a shepherd* (Matthew 9:35-36 GNB).

According to Webster's dictionary, compassion is 'a sympathetic consciousness of another's distress, together with the desire to alleviate it,' Jesus had that kind of compassion.

> *Praise be to God and the Father of our Lord Jesus Christ, the Father of compassion and the God of all comfort, who comforts us in all our troubles, so that we can comfort those in any trouble with the comfort we ourselves have received from God. For just as the sufferings of Christ flow into our lives, so also through Christ our comfort overflows'* (2 Corinthians 1:3-5).

God comforts us so that we in turn can comfort others who are in any trouble. Nothing is too hard for Jesus! Dr. William Barclay, has this to say concerning the word 'comfort'.

> Between verses three and seven of this chapter one of Corinthians the word *comfort* or the verb *to comfort* occurs no fewer than nine times. The word comfort in the New Testament always means far more than soothing sympathy. Always it is true to its root meaning, for its root is the Latin word *fortis,* and *fortis* means *brave.* The Christian comfort is the comfort which brings courage, the comfort which enables

a man to cope with all that life can do to him. Paul was quite sure that God never sends a man a vision without the power to work it out, that God never sends a task without the strength to do it.[29]

Jesus Our Mighty Redeemer

Jesus is the doorway to a new life for us. An opening through the barrier of sin, defeat, despair, sorrow and pain. A way out of bondage and into freedom; out of despair and into hope. A way out of Satan's kingdom and into God's kingdom. Through the cross and the resurrection of Jesus we are set free to begin a new life of victory. Jesus came to release captives from Satan's power (Acts 10:38).

He takes away our sin and makes us into new creations in Christ (2 Corinthians 5:17), he not only forgives our sins but he forgets them once we have asked for forgiveness as we are told by the psalmist –

> *He will not always accuse, nor will he harbour his anger forever; he does not treat us as our sins deserve or repay us according to our iniquities. For as high as the heavens are above the earth, so great is his love for those who fear him; as far as the east is from the west, so far has he removed our transgressions from us* (Psalm 103:9-12).

Jesus The Resurrection and The Life

Jesus said to Martha on his way to bring Lazarus back to life, '*I am the resurrection and the life. He who believes in me will live, even though he dies; and whoever lives and believes in me will never die*' (John 11:25).

---

[29] Barclay, William. *The Daily Study Bible*; The Letters to the Corinthians; The St. Andrew Press; Edinburgh; 1962. Pg. 190

How wonderful for us to know that there is one complete human person in the glory of heaven, Jesus who was crucified and rose again from the dead. He is proof for us that we too will live again.

We know he lives, for he is still carrying on his work of saving, healing, and delivering those who reach out to him in faith.

Conclusion

We can be filled with praise and thanksgiving that Jesus is all of these things. He is the artistic creator, with a holy character, and a healing compassion. He is the mighty conqueror who leads us on to victory, and he is the resurrection and the life!

We can look forward to the eternal life he has promised us as we seek to please him in all that we do (Ephesians 5:10).

Addendum One:

Christ In All The Scriptures

In Genesis he is the blessing of God on all nations.

In Exodus he is the Passover Lamb, and the glory of God in the Tabernacle

In Leviticus he is the Atoning Sacrifice for sin.

In Numbers he is the Brass Snake lifted up, so all who look may live.

He is the Pillar of Cloud by day and the Pillar of Fire by night.

In Deuteronomy he is the Prophet greater than Moses; and the Word of God in our hearts and in our mouths so we can do it.

In Joshua he is the Commander of the army of the Lord.

In Judges he is the Sword of the Lord.

In Ruth he is our Kinsman-Redeemer.

In 1 and 2 Samuel he is the anointed King of Israel.

In 1 and 2 Kings he is the Glory of God in the temple.

In 1 and 2 Chronicles he is the Presence of God in the Ark of the covenant.

In Ezra he is the Restorer of the Church of God.

In Nehemiah he is the Rebuilder of broken walls.

In Esther he is our Saving Intercessor.

In Job he is the Redeemer who lives forever.

In Psalms he is-

the Lord our Shepherd

the King of Glory
the Lord our Light
the Lord our Strength
the Rock of Ages
the Crown of the dynasty of David
a priest forever after the order of Melchizedek
who sits at the right hand of God.
In Proverbs he is the Wisdom of God.
In Ecclesiastes he is the Fear of God.
In the Song of Songs he is
the Shepherd Lover
the Fairest of ten thousand
the Altogether Lovely one.
In Isaiah he is
the Lord of Hosts
Immanuel
Wonderful Counsellor
The Mighty God
The Everlasting Father
The Prince of Peace
The Suffering Servant
The Man of Sorrows
The Anointed Deliverer
In Jeremiah he is the Righteous Branch.
In Lamentations he is the Faithful One.

In Ezekiel he is the Glory of God in the everlasting temple of the prophetic church.

In Daniel he is the Fourth Man in the fiery furnace.

In Hosea he is the faithful Bridegroom.

In Joel he is the Restorer of the lost and the Baptizer in the Holy Spirit.

In Amos he is the Rebuilder of the tent of David.

In Obadiah he is the Gracious Protector.

In Jonah he is the Lord of the Second Chance.

In Micah he is

the Ruler of Israel

God's Law from Zion

and the Lord of peace.

In Nahum he is the Just Avenger.

In Habakkuk he is the God of my salvation.

In Zephaniah he is the Lord of the great Day of God's wrath.

In Haggai he is the Glory of the temple and the Desire of all Nations.

In Zechariah he is the King over all the earth.

In Malachi he is the Sun of Righteousness who rises with healing in his rays.

In Matthew he is the Son of David.

In Mark he is the Son of God.

In Luke he is the Son of Man.

In John he is the great I AM.

In Acts he is the only Name under heaven whereby we must be saved.

In Romans he is the Salvation of God.
In 1 Corinthians he is the Wisdom of God.
In 2 Corinthians he is the Grace of God.
In Galatians he is the Righteousness of God.
In Ephesians he is the Sum of all blessing.
In Philippians he is
the Selfless Servant who-empties himself
humbles himself
takes on human form
becomes obedient to death
is highly exalted
and now has the name above every name
that at the name of Jesus every knee should bow
in heaven, and on earth, and beneath the earth,
and every tongue confess
that Jesus Christ is Lord
to the glory of God the Father
In Colossians he is the Fullness of the Godhead bodily.
In 1 Thessalonians he is the coming Lord of Hope.
In 2 Thessalonians he is the coming Lord of Judgment
In 1 Timothy he is the one Mediator between God and man.
In 2 Timothy he is the Judge of both the living and the dead.
In Titus he is our great God and Saviour.
In Philemon he is our great Liberator.
In Hebrews he is our great High Priest.

In James he is our great Physician.
In 1 Peter he is the great Shepherd and Bishop of our souls.
In 2 Peter he is called His Majesty.
In 1 John he is the Love of God.
In 2 John he is the Truth of God.
In 3 John he is the Goodness of God.
In Jude he is the Lord who comes with ten thousand of his saints.
In Revelation He is the Faithful Witness
the Firstborn from the dead
the Ruler of the kings of the earth
the One who loved us and freed us from our sins
with his own blood
the Coming One
the Son of Man
with eyes like fire
whose feet are like burnished bronze
whose voice is like the sound of many waters
whose word is like a sharp two edged sword
whose face is like the sun
He is the First and the Last
He is the Ever-living One
He holds the keys of death and of hades
He holds the seven stars in his right hand
He walks among the seven churches
He is holy and true

He holds the key of David

He shuts and no one opens; he opens and no one shuts

He is the Amen

and the Ruler of all creation

He is the Lion of the tribe of Judah

He is the Root of David

He is the crucified Lamb

He is the Redeemer of the nations

He is worthy to receive power, riches, wisdom, strength, honour, glory and blessing.

He is the Lord of history

He makes the robes of the saints white with his blood

He is the shepherd of every tribe, nation, people and language

He is the ruler of the nations

He has the Book of Life

He is the Lamb who leads his people

He is the iron-sceptred ruler of the nations

He is the theme of the overcomers' song

He is the heavenly Bridegroom

He is the spirit of prophecy

He is faithful and true

He is the just Warrior

His eyes are like flames of fire

He is crowned with many crowns

He wears a robe dipped in blood

His name is the Word of God

His word is a sharp two-edged sword
He rules the nations with a rod of iron
He treads the winepress of the wrath of God almighty
He is the King of kings!
He is the Lord of lords!
He is the Lamp of heaven
the First and the Last
the Alpha and the Omega
the Beginning and the End
the Root and Offspring of David
the Bright and Morning Star.
HE IS THE LORD JESUS![30]

---

[30] Chant, Barry; Copyright © 2008.

Addendum Two

Strobel, Lee; *The Case for the Real Jesus;* Zondervan; Grand Rapids. Michigan 2007;

Evans, Craig A. *Fabricating Jesus;* 'How Modern Scholars Distort the Gospel'; Downers Grove. lll.: Intervarsity Press; 2006.

Carlson, Stephen C. *The Gospel Hoax:* 'Morton Smith's Invention of Secret Mark'; Waco, Tex.: Baylor University Press; 2005.

Jenkins, Philip; *Hidden Gospels:* 'How the Search for Jesus Lost Its Way'; Oxford University Press; 2001.

Witherington, Ben lll. *What Have They Done With Jesus?;* Harper; San Francisco; 2006.

Wright, N. T. *Judas and the Gospel of Jesus*, Grand Rapids. Mich.: Baker Publishing; 2006.

Bibliography

Josephus, *Antiquities of the Jews;* A. D. 93. 'Translation by William Wiston; Kregel Publications. Grand Rapids. Michigan; 1977.

Tacitus, *Annals* concerning the great fires of Rome (c. A. D. 116)

Youngblood, Ronald F. General Editor; Bruce, F. F. and Harrison, R. K. Consulting Editors; *Nelson's New Illustrated Bible Dictionary*; Reference: 'The Genealogies of Jesus'; Thomas Nelson Publishers; 1995.

Barnes, Albert; *Notes on the New Testament;* Kregel Publications; Grand Rapids. Michigan; 1966.

Pierson, A. T. *The Scriptures:* 'God's Living Oracles'; Pickering & Inglis; London; 1904.

Stoner, Peter & Newman, Robert C. *Science Speaks*; Moody Press; Chicago. Ill.; 1976.

Watts, John D. *World Biblical Commentary* (Isaiah 1-33); Word Books; 1985

Glass, Arthur E. Pamphlet: *'Jeshua in the Tenach'*

Zondervan's *Pictorial Encyclopedia of the Bible*. Reference: 'Quirinius'; Zondervan Publishing; Grand Rapids. Michigan; 1975.

Halley, Henry H. *Halley's Bible Handbook*; Zondervan Publishing; Grand Rapids. Michigan; 1976.

Lockyer, Herbert, *All The Messianic Prophecies of the Bible*; Zondervan Publishing; Grand Rapids. Michigan; 1973.

Newton, John. *A Believer's Progress;* Christian History Magazine, Issue 81.

Gill, John. *Exposition of the Entire Bible*. E Sword; (CD).

Taylor, C. V. From an unpublished work, *The Vision of Isaiah;* 'Christology in Isaiah'.

Baxter, J. Sidlow; *Explore the Book,* 'Volume One'; Published by Marshall Morgan and Scott; 1951.

Vine, W. E. *Expository Dictionary of New Testament Words*; Reference: 'Mediator'.

MacDonald Publishing Co. Virginia; 1969.

Barclay, William. *The Daily Study Bible*; 'The Gospel of John', Volume One. The St. Andrew Press Edinburgh; 1962.

Barclay, William. *The Daily Study Bible*; 'The Letters to the Corinthians'; The St. Andrew Press; Edinburgh; 1962.

Scofield, C. I. The Scofield Reference Bible; Oxford University Press; New York; 1909.

www.ingramcontent.com/pod-product-compliance
Lightning Source LLC
Chambersburg PA
CBHW060521090426
42735CB00011B/2319